First World War
and Army of Occupation
War Diary
France, Belgium and Germany

34 DIVISION
Divisional Troops
74 Sanitary Section
9 January 1916 - 31 March 1917

WO95/2454/2

The Naval & Military Press Ltd
www.nmarchive.com
Published in association with The National Archives

Published by

The Naval & Military Press Ltd

Unit 10 Ridgewood Industrial Park,

Uckfield, East Sussex,

TN22 5QE England

Tel: +44 (0) 1825 749494

www.naval-military-press.com

www.nmarchive.com

This diary has been reprinted in facsimile from the original. Any imperfections are inevitably reproduced and the quality may fall short of modern type and cartographic standards.

© Crown Copyright
Images reproduced by permission of The National Archives, London, England, 2015.

Contents

Document type	Place/Title	Date From	Date To
Heading	WO95/2454/2		
Heading	34th Division 74th Sanitary Section 1916 Jan-1917 Apl		
Heading	34th Div 74th Sany Section Jan 1916-Dec 16		
War Diary	Sutton Veny	09/01/1916	09/01/1916
War Diary	Southampton Water	10/01/1916	10/01/1916
War Diary	On Train	11/01/1916	11/01/1916
War Diary	Argues	12/01/1916	16/01/1916
War Diary	La Crosse	17/01/1916	22/01/1916
War Diary	Morbecque	23/01/1916	31/01/1916
Heading	P O 74 Sanitary Section Feb March April 1916		
Heading	War Diary Of 74th Sanitary Section 34th Division From Feby 1st 1916 To Feb 29th 1916 Vol. 2		
War Diary	Morbecque	01/02/1916	03/02/1916
War Diary	Croix Du Bac	04/02/1916	11/02/1916
War Diary	Morbecque	13/02/1916	23/02/1916
War Diary	Croix Du Bac	24/02/1916	29/02/1916
Heading	War Diary Of 74th Sanitary Section Mar 1916. Vol 3		
War Diary	Croix Du Bac	01/03/1916	31/03/1916
Heading	War Diary Of O/C 74th Sanitary Section 34th Division April 1916 Vol No 4		
War Diary	Croix Du Bac	01/04/1916	19/04/1916
War Diary	Tilques	10/04/1916	26/04/1916
Heading	War Diary Of 74th Sanitary Section May 1916 Vol 5		
War Diary	Tilques	05/05/1916	05/05/1916
War Diary	Bresle	06/05/1916	08/05/1916
War Diary	Behencourt	09/05/1916	31/05/1916
Heading	War Diary Of O/C 74th Sanitary Section 34th Division June 1916 Pages 7 Vol. 6		
War Diary	Behencourt	01/06/1916	23/06/1916
War Diary	Albert	24/06/1916	29/06/1916
War Diary	Moulin Du Vivier	30/06/1916	30/06/1916
Heading	War Diary Of 74th Sanitary Section From July 1st 1916 To July 31st 1916 (Volume 7)		
War Diary	Moulin Du Vivier	01/07/1916	03/07/1916
War Diary	Baizieux	04/07/1916	07/07/1916
War Diary	Albert	08/07/1916	19/07/1916
War Diary	Baizieux	20/07/1916	30/07/1916
War Diary	Albert	31/07/1916	31/07/1916
Heading	War Diary Of O/C 74th Sanitary Section For August 1916 Volume No. 8 Pages 5		
War Diary	Albert	01/08/1916	13/08/1916
War Diary	Baizieux	14/08/1916	17/08/1916
War Diary	Hallencourt	18/08/1916	20/08/1916
War Diary	Doulieu	21/08/1916	23/08/1916
War Diary	Croix Du Bac	24/08/1916	31/08/1916
Heading	War Diary Of O/C 74th Sanitary Section 34th Division September 1916 Vol No. 9. Pages 4		
War Diary	Croix Du Bac	01/09/1916	30/09/1916
Heading	War Diary Of O/C 74th Sanitary Section 34th Division. Vol No. 10 Pages 4 October 1916		

War Diary	Croix Du Bac	01/10/1916	24/10/1916
Heading	War Diary Of O/C 74th Sanitary Section November-1916 Vol. 11 Pages. Vol XI.		
War Diary	Croix Du Bac	03/11/1916	30/11/1916
Heading	34th Div. War Diary Of O/C 74th Sanitary Section December 1916 Volume XII Pages 5		
War Diary	Croix Du Bac	01/12/1916	31/12/1916
Heading	34th Div. War Diary Of O/C 74th Sanitary Section January 1917 Vol. XII Pages 5		
War Diary	Croix Du Bac	01/01/1917	26/01/1917
War Diary	Fletre	27/01/1917	31/01/1917
Heading	34th Div. War Diary Of O/C 74th Sanitary Section For February 1917 Volume XIV Pages 4		
War Diary	Fletre	01/02/1917	18/02/1917
War Diary	Hermaville	19/02/1917	28/02/1917
Heading	War Diary Of O/C 74th Sanitary Section For March 1917 Vol. 2 Pages 6 No. 15. Vol 2		
War Diary	Hermaville	01/03/1917	31/03/1917

WD55/2454(2)

WD55/2454(2)

34TH DIVISION

74TH SANITARY SECTION

~~JAN - DEC 1916~~
1916 JAN — 1917 APL

TO 3 ARMY

Sam: Sect: 74
Vol: I
Jan 15/6

34

34 th Div.

34 Div

4th Sany. Sector

Jan 14th
–
Dec '16

Army Form C. 2118.

WAR DIARY
or
INTELLIGENCE SUMMARY.
(Erase heading not required.)

Sheet No. 1.

Instructions regarding War Diaries and Intelligence Summaries are contained in F.S. Regs., Part II. and the Staff Manual respectively. Title pages will be prepared in manuscript.

[Stamp: 74th SANITARY SECTION * 34th DIVISION]

Place	Date	Hour	Summary of Events and Information	Remarks and references to Appendices
Sutton Veny	Jan 9 1916	7 p.m.	Load Lorry (Motor) in charge of Cap.t White FPS Arun (and Graham) was despatched from Sutton Veny at 5.30 a.m. Arrived at Southampton Docks at 11.30 a.m.	
Southampton Docks	Jan 10 1916	8 a.m.	Left Sutton Veny at 8.45. Marched to Warminster, where the Section, consisting of 2 S.N.C.Os. Men 70 men Lorries entrained with myself. Arrived Warminster 10.20 a.m. Entrained Southampton Docks 12.30 p.m. Embarked S.S. Matheran 3.30 p.m. With Cap.t White on the 2 Priors reported - Left Southampton 5 p.m.	
On Train	Jan 11 mid-night 1916		Arrived Port of Havre at 4.30 a.m. Disembarked 3.30 p.m. Entrained Motor Lorry & 1 or. Ambulance motors afterwards - Proceeded to Brick Rest Camp at 5.30 p.m. Arrived at 6 p.m. Returned at Point 1 at 9 p.m. Reported at Havre at 11.59 - Motor Lorry in charge of Cap.t White - 12 Prior was left at Havre pursuant to instructions from Col. White at Hotel de Ville.	
Etaples	Jan 12 10 p.m. 1916		Arrived St Omer at 6 p.m. Men intended to go to train. I proceeded to train at 6.30 with Interpreter requested Billet for self & men, being turn out at St Omer by Major Barba (when I report). RTO 24 R.C.Os. men with our horse at 9 p.m. in Market Square of Etaples. Marched them to their quarters -	
Etaples	Jan 13 7 p.m. 1916		Inspected Section 9 a.m. - Inspected Equipment. At 2 p.m. Met to Principal Headquarters at la Crosse Mohaly-Haltie.S.	
Etaples	Jan 14 7 p.m. 1916		Section went for routemarch 9.15 a.m. took to Renescure HQrs Instructions from 101st Coy R.S.C. as our ration had not arrived owing to breakdown in the transport Arranged by etc.	

Army Form C. 2118.

WAR DIARY
or
INTELLIGENCE SUMMARY.
(Erase heading not required.)

Sheet No. 2.

[Stamp: 74th SANITARY SECTION / 34th DIVISION]

Place	Date	Hour	Summary of Events and Information	Remarks and references to Appendices
Argues	Jan 14 1916	7 p.m.	At 2.30 p.m. rode to Headquarters. Reported to D.D.M.S. that Sister Lorry on road outside Headquarters at 2/4/1912 Motor lorry arrived Argues at 2.30 p.m. Sergt. White reported that he left Havre in charge of this transport on Jan 12th – 15 Manchester at 4 p.m. where he reported by telegram D.D.M.S. at Abbeville. Left Abbeville at 8.25 a.m. on 13th Jan. 16 reached Abbeville at 2.30 p.m. Reported to Commander Stationed Base to D.D.M.S. Abbeville. Left Abbeville at 9.30 a.m. 12th Jan. 16.	
Argues	Jan 15 1916	7 p.m.	Proceeded to Wardrecques on Sister day for rations then went to Divisional Headquarters, reported to D.D.M.S. Section went for route march. Gave all members of Section an extra Stripe (without pay) have taken on Subs. with their respective units. V.S.	
Argues	Jan 16 1916	7 p.m.	Inspected Section – full march order. Part three special in character inspection – Huts, troops on Billetfarm on Kittelfarm Bay. Rest of Headquarters in afternoon or taw – D.M.S.	
La Crosse	Jan 17 1916	7 p.m.	Attached Reserve Squad of their respective units – Heathrow Division of streets on Motor Lorry. Proceeded with Sergt-Major Parris to St. Omer reported to Col. Watt R.A.C., who gave us much useful information on Sanitary matters. Returned to Argues at 2.15 P.M. 3.45 went to Divisional Headquarters, the Sanitary Squad attached to Divisional Headquarters proceed on the Motor Lorry to the same Place, where troops detailed with Public Veterinary Section. Reported to A.D.S.	

Army Form C. 2118.

Sheet No 3

WAR DIARY
or
INTELLIGENCE SUMMARY.
(Erase heading not required.)

[Stamp: 74TH SANITARY SECTION / 34th DIVISION]

Place	Date	Hour	Summary of Events and Information	Remarks and references to Appendices
La Crosse	Jan 18 1916	7 p.m.	Inspected Divisional Headquarters area – Continued Incinerator. Construction carried out – Water Supply tested by Horrocks test. Found 1/2 lb of [good quality] hyp. [sufficient] area occupied by Public Veterinary Section. Made orders for construction of incinerators. Short trench latrines in a suitable situation.	
La Croix	19.1.16	7 p.m.	Rode to Staple Mollen Cappel – Inspected areas occupied by 20th C.S.R.E., 15th Sqdn 12 Hudden, 16th Royal Scots. Found that the water was drawn from wells [that] had not been tested with Horrocks test – arranged for this to be done.	
La Croix	20.1.16	7 p.m.	Went with Major B.B. Burke R.N.C. & Badical & Saw Captain Smale (Sanitary Officer) who found an incinerator [illegible] which had been made under his direction from kerosene [illegible] which was successfully coping with [from 50 – 100 tons of refuse] daily (i.e. from a Civil Population of 1500). A cart party of [troops]. Captain Smale also [shewed] a number of in [previous] Sanitary arrangement made from [incinerator] [illegible] & practiced in the F.W.	
La Croix	21.1.16	7 p.m.	Rode to Renescure Monthergnat. Inspected quarters of 15th Royal Scots – 102nd [Field Ambulance] – 11th Suffolks – 205 C.S.R.E., T20, 21, 22, T23 who with [illegible] – Found that the water from wells were in some instances [illegible] and without [illegible] or disinfectant. Gave orders that all water had to be tested by Horrocks test.	

2353 Wt. W2544/1454 700,000 5/15 D. D. & L. A.D.S.S./Forms/C. 2118.

WAR DIARY / INTELLIGENCE SUMMARY

Army Form C. 2118.

74th Sanitary Section, 34th Division

Place	Date	Hour	Summary of Events and Information	Remarks
La Crow	21.1.16	7 p.m.	[to] Theatre, otherwise [idle]	
La Crow	22.1.16	7.30 p.m.	Rode (J.A. & I) Motorcycle to 5th (?) from O.C. Sean. Sec. 33 of 20th Division on "Route" in Lorry "11" [illegible]. Thank Divisioners. Returned to Divisional Headquarters. Inspected Scene. Various squads of Sanitary Section reported at Orderly Room at 9.30. Received pay. Afterwards spoke the Senior N.C.O's. This award raises point in their report that there is certain report / future report. Officer turned this fraction.	A.7.
Montecques	23.1.16	10 p.m.	Rode Motorcycle (10.30 a.m.) for number of Section. To Hinxin (Saga Major Ronti in charge) there on leave. Inter Army — arrived Montecques 12.30. Met up with our question in Horse Met had few vacates on the Interior. Pay by Sanitary Officer of 20th Division. M.E.	
Montecques	24.1.16	7.30 p.m.	Rode to La Belle Hotesse. Saw N.O. of 102nd Ambulance Various Medical matters [illegible] water supply Inspine Hospital write him. Rode After. Went back to Rumberques. Visited areas occupied by 11th Suffolk 7 10.45 Field Ambulance, etc. occupied by 102nd Ambulance – 11th Suffolks, their water supply from Standpipe on. Montecques – Harlebrook road on side of Rumberques. Visited the Hospital [illegible]	
Montecques	25.1.16	10 p.m.	Went to Skinberque [illegible] trees [illegible] of R.E. Stores, General supplies, [illegible] Sandbags in elton [illegible] In the afternoon inspected area occupied by 101st F.A. & 102nd F. Ambulance + 10th L[illegible]	7

Army Form C. 2118.

Sheet No 5

WAR DIARY
or
INTELLIGENCE SUMMARY.
(Erase heading not required.)

Place	Date	Hour	Summary of Events and Information	Remarks and references to Appendices
Montreuil	26.1.16	7 p.m.	Rode Blorie (seen reported batteries at Headquarters. Visited Camp & bivouacs of Train, Schutt an outhouse used as an "abattoir" in Blorie — Plans for Manufacts. clothing with Clayton — Corporal Shilton $\frac{1}{8}$/71st San. Sec. British his left humerus has required total — R.D. Ambulance at Montreuil.	
Montreuil	27.1.16	10 p.m.	Rode to Serras. Visited Camp, Stables & of 2/1 Northumberland Inniskn. F.S. 26th R.T. — endeavoured to have an inspection. Arrangements in Serras installed for disinfecting clothing, but was not successful — Visited small scattered patches of Squadron, A.S.C. F.25=9.T at Serras, $\frac{1}{2}$ La Belle Hôtesse.	
Montreuil	28.1.16	6.30 p.m.	Rode hard 250 Manhist from 2/1st Northumberland Patch at No. 4 F.M. Ambulance in the Thirtill Amphies Rode to Strazeele $\frac{1}{3}$ 102, Blainfleur, The Belle Hôtesse. Inspected Water Master Supply of 162 $\frac{2}{3}$ B? R.F.A. Morrison. Headquarters + of B.T.C (billeting of $\frac{1}{176}$ Bs R.F.A.) Reported at Masse Orderly room had food time sub [BS.	
Montreuil	29.1.16	7.30 p.m.	Rode to Steenbecque. Visited Camps of 2/2nd + 2/5th Northumberland Fus." inspected them with M.Os - Interviewed billets of Mobile Veterinary Section, T B Section of 102 Field Ambulance - Inspt A.D.M.S. in Strazeele. Piers out him to Blainfleur. Preferred without repairs in institution of measures of members of 74/ San Sec. Subsequent Division — In afternoon rode with Fortis & Witter re-subs. Sam, $\frac{1}{3}$ $\frac{1}{176}$ R.F.A. Lt.	
Montreuil	30.1.16		Attended correspondence etc in Orderly room in morning — In afternoon went to Estaire Montreuil and R.C. Os. in Charge of Sanitation of 102nd Infantry Bo Hof. & Intervened Pumoratous Fr. Oliven B7.	

Army Form C. 2118.

WAR DIARY
or
INTELLIGENCE SUMMARY.
(Erase heading not required.)

Place	Date	Hour	Summary of Events and Information	Remarks and references to Appendices
Montreque	31.1.16	8.30a	R&R 6 Scories Thingfield various billets of 2.6th North umberland Fusiliers with Lieut Perris R.A.M.C. inspt 152 W-B.M R.F.A. at Ayet Hernuel Sanitary arrangements at Ughton Return. Proceed to Blairs-Sur-Tinchiets hid normal inspection. B.M.C. (area of Divisional Train instruction) to Corporal Howard (Ju.K.an.k.) also in inspection with him the area occupied by a section of 10495 Rich ambulance. Reports of Officers issued as Divisions have been.	

M Grant Lieut R.M.C
74th SANITARY SECTION.

Feb
March } 1916
April

S.S.U. 7th Sanitary Section

34th Div

Feb 1916

Confidential

War Diary
of
1/4th Sanitary Section
34th Division

From Feby 1st 1916 to Feb 29th 1916

Vol. 2.

7 Sheets

WAR DIARY or INTELLIGENCE SUMMARY

Army Form C. 2118.

(Erase heading not required.)

Place	Date	Hour	Summary of Events and Information	Remarks and references to Appendices
MORBECQUE	1.11.16	7.45 a.m	Cap⁰ MESSENT Robt. C.T. Sanitary Officer of 23rd Division called & issued Sanitary matter – went with me & inspected R.E. Headquarters, Billets – Went in afternoon to ESTAIRE, & saw 2/L HARRIS JONES M.O. of 34th Div: & his Column – discussed the treatment of water & other matters & subsequently inspected one of the billets. (In Subsequently obtained O.P.S.)	
MORBECQUE	2.11.16	8.30 a.m.	Dealt with correspondence – Received orders to arrange to take on the 7th & Sany Sec: Feb 4th to 1916 to CROIX DU BAC to be attached for 4 days in tradition with 23rd Division. Met at that end of 4 days thereabout was to be relieved by the transverse div of 74th Sany Sec. Became one of 5 waterparty men of 175th Bn. R.F.A. in other spare units for water & other Rode in afternoon to FIELD CASHIER for money. May seen – afterwards to billets of 230th – 232nd Coys O.P.S. M.S.C. Saw M.O. Lieut CARNES & issued the water supply of 232nd Coy M.S.C. in those billets a well had been contained as unfit for drink: I their supply drawn from a better source.	O.R.
MORBECQUE	3.11.16	6 p.m.	Rode to LA BELLE HOTESSE & STEENBECQUE & inspected billets & installment of 122nd Field Ambulance, 27th North'd Fus: Bn & Camp of 28th Notts Fusilier. Wire forwarded to BLARINGHEM report D.A.D.M.S. Paid Sen ot men: proceeded from AIRE & saw Corporal Ashford in 22nd Casualty Clearing Hospital	O.R.

Army Form C. 2118.

WAR DIARY
or
INTELLIGENCE SUMMARY.
(Erase heading not required.)

Instructions regarding War Diaries and Intelligence Summaries are contained in F.S. Regs., Part II. and the Staff Manual respectively. Title pages will be prepared in manuscript.

Place	Date	Hour	Summary of Events and Information	Remarks and references to Appendices
CROIX DU BAC	4.11.16	9pm	Proceeded in motor lorry with clerks, R.C.O., PR, Jnr, Sgn. Sec. to CROIX DU BAC. Motor attached to Sani. Section of 23rd Division for instruction. — Reported to A.D.M.S. of 34th Division at CROIX DU BAC. Motor lorry returned to MORBECQUE same evening.	OK.
CROIX DU BAC	5.11.16	7pm	Went with Captain MESSENT O.C. of 25th Divisional Sanitary Section to ERQUINGHEM LYS. Inspected town. Farms occupied by troops. Ar(tillery) m(en) of 76th Sanitary Section with cinemas by 23rd Divisional Sani. Sec. for instruction in latrin attached lectures in afternoon. at BAC ST MAUR on outskirts of town which was followed by a most interesting discussion.	OK.
CROIX DU BAC	6.11.16	7pm	Went with Capt. MESSENT to various camps. Tollett and CROIX DU BAC.	OK.
CROIX DU BAC	7.11.16	7pm	Went with Capt MESSENT to ERQUINGHEM LYS, GRIS POT, & ARMENTIERES in cars. Visited various camps & barns occupied by troops, also the billeting of Batts at ERQUINGHEM, where they are billeted with upwards of 2000 men per barn — given hot baths, though of uncertainty. That evening twenty of drinks when veneers are. In afternoon visits various camps. Tollett at various STEENWERCK.	OK.
CROIX DU BAC	8.11.16	7pm	Went to ERQUINGHEM LYS & L'EPINETTE. Examined various Camps. Prescribed areas. In afternoon witnessed tank recently occupied by Transport of 11th Suffolk at RUE DORMOIRE & found it in a very filthy condition. Subsection of 76th Sani Sec. from CROIX DU BAC employed there clearing them.	OK.

WAR DIARY
or
INTELLIGENCE SUMMARY.
(Erase heading not required.)

Army Form C. 2118.

Remarks and references to Appendices

3

Place	Date	Hour	Summary of Events and Information	Remarks
CROIX DU BAC	9.11.16	7 pm	Visit ERQUINGHEM LYS, GRIS POT & RUE DU BIE — visited various camps. — ERQUINGHEM LYS & BAC ST MAUR were shelled this morning.	OR
CROIX DU BAC	10.11.16	7 pm	Visit ERQUINGHEM LYS & ARMENTIERES — saw 2/Lt BROWN of 36th — saw in morning. Visited afternoon to STEENWERCK — LE PETIT MORTIER — visit various camps & BSM &c	OR
CROIX DU BAC	11.11.16	7 pm	Visit ERQUINGHEM LYS in morning. In afternoon (second) various administrative details with Captain MESSENT.	OR
MORBECQUE	12.11.16	9 pm	Visit ERQUINGHEM LYS in morning. In afternoon returned to MORBECQUE in new Zone HQ	
MORBECQUE	13.11.16	8 pm	Rode to BLARINGHEM — visited DADMS 34th Division — In afternoon visited Camp at STEENBECQUE — vacated that morning by 22nd Northumberland Fusiliers. Found it in a very unsatisfactory condition — also visited billets [?] in same place vacated that morning by 20th Northumberland Fusiliers. Found them satisfactory with the 2nd Withers accommodation for incoming troops. — Reports with ADMS 34th Division	OR
MORBECQUE	14.11.16	9 pm	Visited camp in the morning by 23rd Northumberland Fusiliers — 21st Northumberland Fusiliers in afternoon. Satisfied the latter. Rode to HQ ADMS 31st Division. RH to BLARINGHEM — saw ADMS — Visited water supply & divisional Headquarters. In afternoon rode to LES CISEAUX — visited various Adv. troops [?]	OR

Place	Date	Hour	Summary of Events and Information	Remarks and references to Appendices
			occupied by 18th Northumberland Fusiliers among whom there has been an outbreak of Paratyphoid Fever (5 cases) — Found Mortuary (which was placed "out of bounds" first in circular letter of 28.12. Division (Sherwood Foresters) had been acquainted of that, had been re occupied form	4
MORBECQUE 15.1.16	4 pm		Rode to SERCUS — LA BELLE HOTESSE & STEENBECQUE in morn. Visited various billets in a camp recently occupied by 10.3.2 Infantry Bde — found them in a satisfactory condition with a humane exceptions allowed. Due to inclement rain early no fatigues have been (till then) of clear up. In the afternoon visited Camp & billets occupied by 15th & 16th Royal Scots, 10th Lincolns, 11th Suffolks. I after transport of personnel at MORBECQUE. Found the generality in fairly satisfactory condition but not having (been in accordance with Divisional Order except the care of the 16th Royal Scots — made arrangements with Divisional supply for the re mounted property to ADMS	WI
MORBECQUE 16.1.16	9 pm		Rode BLARINGHEM — reported to ADMS, visited Camp recently vacated by 21st Battn Northum'b'd & secured sanitary reports — sat with M.O. of 23rd Divisional Unit now in occupation. In afternoon walked to STEENBECQUE — saw Ms of 23rd Divisional Units occupying Camps vacated by 22nd & 28th Northumberland Fusiliers. Arranged to send N.C.Os of 72nd San Sec in turn for Sanitary in turn in permanent in Camps	WI

Army Form C. 2118.

WAR DIARY
or
INTELLIGENCE SUMMARY.
(Erase heading not required.)

5

Place	Date	Hour	Summary of Events and Information	Remarks and references to Appendices
MORBECQUE	11.11.16	10 p.m.	Rode BLARINGHEM, WITTES & LYNDE – Inspected Billet Areas recently vacated by 152nd, 160th, 175th, & 176th Bde. R.F.A. – Scout report to C.O. M.S. 3rd Division – Motor Lorry sent to A.S.C. workshops for overhaul. Thanked with Divisional Head, another Lorry for transportography R.B.	
MORBECQUE	15.11.16	7.30 p.s.	Attended to various correspondence – rode to Field Cashier – Drew 460 francs for pay of my Section. Forwarded tomorrow from A.S.C. & Lorry of Motor Lorry dismissed – Visited troops of 104th Field Ambulance at MORBECQUE, also certain billets of 16th Royal Scots – several parts of MORBECQUE.	W.S.
MORBECQUE	19.11.16	5.30 p.m.	Rode AIRE – Saw Corporal ASHFORD 11th Sanitary Section – returning as States away on Tuesday next 22.11.16. from there to BLARINGHEM – WITTES – Inspected watersupply of Troops. Rode & afterwards to BLARINGHEM. Reported to A.D.M.S. – Went with him & visited reinforcements by Numa of 176th Bde R.F.A. at B.	W.S.
MORBECQUE	20.11.16	6 p.m.	Sent to 2 Cos. of Section at CROIX DU BAC & ERQUINGHEM to look up areas of troops – Inspected Camps & Billets vacated yesterday 19.11.16 by 15th & 76th Royal Scots, 10th Lincolns & 11th Suffolks – Brigade open latrine pits for latrine practice the left behind their areas was in a generally satisfactory condition – reported same to A.D.M.S.	W.S.
MORBECQUE	21.11.16	10.30 p.m.	Rode BLARINGHEM – rode to STEENBECQUE – Inspected Camps & Billets occupied by 21st, 22nd Northumberlands –	W.S.

2353 Wt. W2544/1454 700,000 5/15 D. D. & L. A.D.S.S./Forms/C. 2118.

WAR DIARY
INTELLIGENCE SUMMARY

Army Form C. 2118.

Place	Date	Hour	Summary of Events and Information	Remarks and references to Appendices
MORBECQUE	22.11.16	7.30 a	Rode BLARINGHEM & saw ADMS - arrange return visits prior to leaving for CROIX DU BAC in morn. Afternoon Dum - Found billets for Sanitary Section of 23rd Division at MORBECQUE - also at BLARINGHEM. Sentenced Private STRITCH who was attached from ASC 4/Pun. S.C. for duty with Portable Army Disinfector, 6.2 Days C.B. & Forfeiture of pay for 2 Days.	OK.
MORBECQUE	23.11.16	7.30 a	Order for move cancelled - Visits various Camps & billets around MORBECQUE and BLARINGHEM Saw ADMS.	OK
CROIX DU BAC	24.11.16	9 h	Rode to CROIX DU BAC & other available hospitals ADMS - Auto Lorry came over with various members of Sector & some stores.	OK
CROIX DU BAC	25.11.16	7.30 a	Visits STEENWERCKE manured & Comms - Call from Deputy Mayor - Inspector present all that & went to billets around CROIX DU BAC. Lorry went to previous HQ for OK	OK
CROIX DU BAC	26.11.16	7.30 a	Visits BAC ST MAUR & ERQUINGHEM in morn - BAC ST MAUR, ERQUINGHEM L'EPINETTE in afternoon - Inspected billets of Irish Rifle Horse at BAC ST MAUR (Mascot) GUN Ammunition (829 bi(L)) APM - arrange for loan of cart for Securing unit fatigues at L'EPINETTE	OK
CROIX DU BAC	27.11.16	7 h	Visits STEENWERCKE in morn - Called at billets of RAMC Veterinary Section, 160th RFA &	

Army Form C. 2118.

WAR DIARY
or
INTELLIGENCE SUMMARY.
(Erase heading not required.)

Instructions regarding War Diaries and Intelligence Summaries are contained in F.S. Regs., Part II and the Staff Manual respectively. Title pages will be prepared in manuscript.

Place	Date	Hour	Summary of Events and Information	Remarks and references to Appendices
CROIX DU BAC	28.11.16	10.30 a.m.	176th R.F.A. In afternoon visited camps of 20th & 23rd Northumberland Fusiliers. O/R. Rode ERQUINGHEM in morning, visited camps, billets of 23rd Northumberland Fusiliers with M.O. Two civilians at ERQUINGHEM – Paul civilian at CROIX DU BAC nr. STEENWERCK[?] a fatale [?]. visited billets of Motor Transport, 102nd Field Ambulance. Paid visit to have 176 Br R.F.A. Sprayed. 5 billets of Motor Transport with Paraffin. Paid civilian at STEENWERCK. O/R.	
CROIX DU BAC	29.11.16	8 p.m.	Rode to ERQUINGHEM — visited camps of 23rd & 20th Northumberland Fusiliers — reoccupied with 20 o/s to spray out huts — revisited camps — also visited Hospitals of 101st Fd[?] R.I. in same locality. Camps & billets of 22nd Northumberland Fusiliers, + the billets of 161st R.I. + Motor hand[?] que station at CROIX DU BAC. Issued O/R for certain Sanitary improvements. Sent sprays in charge of N.C.O. to billets occupied by Indian hawkers que station of 175th R.F.A. O/R.	

M Edward ? Lt. (T.F.)

2353 Wt. W2544/1454 700,000 5/15 D.D.&L. A.D.S.S./Forms/C. 2118.

34th Div.

Confidential

WAR - DIARY

of

7th. SANITARY SECTION.

Nov 1916

74 San Sec
Vol 3

Army Form C. 2118.

Sheet No 1

WAR DIARY
or
INTELLIGENCE SUMMARY.
(Erase heading not required.)

Place	Date	Hour	Summary of Events and Information	Remarks and references to Appendices
CROIX DU BAC	1.iii.16	9 p.m.	Examined 2 water points run by 17 & 18th R.F.A. rapport after for water duty. Both STEENWERCKE rain pits billets & bath of 103rd Field Ambulance. Sprayed huts billets occupied by 23rd Northumbr[ian] Fusiliers - both in afternoon. FORT ROMPU rainwater on platform & say — provided STEERQUINGHEM rainwater area occupied by 20 Coy R.E. rainwater for water supply — had never water supplies & improved since area occupied by Flotilla a (?) for 7 months (presently received amount of first-aid). Visited billets that occupied by Northumbs Gun Section (Flo) hut in which Section is erected. Sprayed with creol. Inspect. various repositions on Sanitary matters, also visited billet occupied by Div. R.A.	C/R
CROIX DU BAC	2.iii.16	11 a.m.	Visited STEENWERCKE resolved difficulties with civilian labourers - called on ADMS of 9th Division. Some of these huts were rainproofed billets in town afternoon to work in conjunction with San. Officer of 9th Division. Visited NIEPPE & onward train thence to (for both of) STEENWERCKE on to ERQUINGHEM & ARMENTIERES rainproofed for cleaning of cesspools with contractor. In afternoon visited camp billet occupied by 18th 170th R.F.A. on road between CROIX DU BAC & STEENWERCKE rainproof. (W various Sanitary matters with COs of Coys. Proceeded with paraffin spraying of billets - huts, & rainwater supply. Both. C/R	

WAR DIARY or INTELLIGENCE SUMMARY

Army Form C. 2118.

Place	Date	Hour	Summary of Events and Information	Remarks and references to Appendices
CROIX DU BAC	3.iii.16	11.30pm	Rct ERQUINGHEM — inspected billet occupied by 207th Coy R.E. — Sappers also 105th Field Ambulance — Billet occupied by 209th Coy R.E. — T36b—27th Northumberland Fusiliers in afternoon — Received Sanitary reports with No. Os at CHAPELLE ARMENTIERE, also visited Dressing Stations of 104th Field Ambulance at same place — Also visited 160th & 161st R.F.A. Hqrs. Mosquito certain sanitary matters.	WS
CROIX DU BAC	4.iii.16	11pm	Rct STEENWERCKE — inspected Baths of 103rd Field Ambulance, saw C.O. — arranged for supply of supplies — Visited various areas in STEENWERCKE — In afternoon visited Camps & Billets of 152nd Bde R.F.A. also 2 Col. also of Divisional Amn. Column — reports conditions satisfactory to O.C.	CAT CAT
CROIX DU BAC	5.iii.16	11pm	Inspected Camps & Billets vacated by 20th, 21st, 22nd, 23rd North'd Fus'rs in previous day, reports on conditions to A.D.M.S. — Inspected Guard's Billet at BAC ST MAUR, conferred of Squad Health & Water.	CAT
CROIX DU BAC	6.iii.16	8.p.m.	Rct ERQUINGHEM — inspected two new Hospitals small unit situates, Pm afternoon had interview at CROIX DU BAC Farm — to billet future ERQUINGHEM — L'EPINETTE occupied by B.Bde (wagon lines) of 75th Bde R.F.A. when the cases of pneumonia had recently occurred — had place thoroughly cleansed out & sprayed with cresol — also a STEENWERCKE had interview — Paid a visit to 7th San. Sec. V.R.	WS
CROIX DU BAC	7.iii.16	7.45pm	Rct BAC ST MAUR — inspected Canteen T.Y.M.C.A. hut — Gouvernement — undetermined arrangt for transport — Hunt to ERQUINGHEM, ROLANDERIE FARM, GRIS POT, L'ARMEE & RUE MARLE inspected Billets & camps occupied by 11th Suffolks, 207th — Coy R.E. + 20th T.R.I. Northumberland Fusiliers, the accepted capital at ERQUINGHEM.	WS

Army Form C. 2118.

WAR DIARY
or
INTELLIGENCE SUMMARY.
(Erase heading not required.)

Instructions regarding War Diaries and Intelligence Summaries are contained in F.S. Regs., Part II. and the Staff Manual respectively. Title pages will be prepared in manuscript.

3

Place	Date	Hour	Summary of Events and Information	Remarks and references to Appendices
CROIX DU BAC	8.iii.16	9 p.m.	Rode L'EPINETTE where sent for incinerator storm have manure, to the [from Armentières] in afternoon camp occupied by/an lines of 175th R.F.A. Rode to L'ESTRATE visited Rest camp of 102nd F.d Ambulance — In afternoon rode to ERGUINGHEM ARMENTIÈRES visited billet occupied by Pioneers of 16th Anti-Aircraft Section — 20th Field Ambce Sn In__, & R.E. Sect at R.E. Dump.	
CROIX DU BAC	9.iii.16	11 a.m.	Rode CHAPELLE ARMENTIÈRES visited billet occupied by 2nd C.B.R. & 2nd Essex. Battalion and Pavilion [illegible] A.D.S. of each unit. Inspected latter Sanitary structure. In afternoon rode to ROLANDERIE FARM & RUE DELATRE visited billets & Camps of 11th Suffolks, 10th Lincolns, 15th Royal Scots Fusiliers and C.O. of same.	
CROIX DU BAC	10.iii.16	11 a.m.	Inspected cesspit at back of HdQrs (Bde) at CROIX DU BAC — rode STEENWERCKE en route visited review occupied by [illegible] with drain for their emptying, also inspected 2 cesspits at Hospital of 103rd F.d. Ambulance at STEENWERCKE; visited drains Ur__of 176th R.F.A., Public Util: Sec, & A.Battery 160th R.F.A. Mess, W[ ] for spraying of hutments billets with paraffin. Rode in afternoon to ERGUINGHEM Rev[] area occupied by 102nd F.d Ambulance, 207th Coy R.E., & 160th R.F.A — Selected site for erection of Showbaths at CROIX DU BAC. Visited Camps occupied by 24 & 26th Divn Pavilion at the Review with R.O.C.	
CROIX DU BAC	11.iii.16	11 a.m.	Rode ARMENTIÈRES Arrangements for emptying cesspits at CROIX DU BAC, STEENWERCKE, & ERGUINGHEM Rnd civilian labourers — Paid civilians at CROIX DU BAC, Rode to LA ROSSIGNOL & selected site for Shower Baths for a Company A.S.C., & that area — inspected their Camp, billets. Paid civilians at STEENWERCKE.	

2353 Wt. W2544/1454 700,000 5/15 D. D. & L. A.D.S.S./Forms/C. 2118.

Army Form C. 2118.

WAR DIARY
or
INTELLIGENCE SUMMARY.
(Erase heading not required.)

Instructions regarding War Diaries and Intelligence Summaries are contained in F. S. Regs., Part II. and the Staff Manual respectively. Title pages will be prepared in manuscript.

Place	Date	Hour	Summary of Events and Information	Remarks and references to Appendices
CROIX DU BAC	12.iii.16	11½a	Went with Major BURKE, DADMS 24th Div to CHAPELLE ARMENTIERES, L'ARMEE & RUE DELATREE r/visited Elliot Camps of 22nd Northumberland Fusiliers, 205th Coy R.E., & 15th Royal Scots, also attached Motor Station of 104th Field Ambulance — in afternoon r/visited Horse Lines of 152nd Bde R.F.A. shown lit., & of A.F.C. Batteries of 160th Bde R.F.A.	OK
CROIX DU BAC	13.iii.16	11.45a	Rode L'EPINETTE & looked out ground for central Divisional Incinerators; in afternoon r/visited ERQUINGHEM & FORT ROMPU, r/visited Elliot & Salvage Coy r/started a stand for incinerator attendants in huts, Camps of B & C Batteries of 152nd Bde R.F.A., D & E Batteries of 76th Brit'l Pavilion	OK
CROIX DU BAC	14.iii.16	11½a	Rode L'EPINETTE & selected construction of incinerator for Central Dump, r/visit Elliot of B By 175th R.F.A. When a outbreak of Influenza has occurred intervened and supplied necessary extras, paid Ellot r/side arrangements for securing & voiding of LEPINETTE. In afternoon r/visited Elliot C. Major BURKE & LEPINETTE r/visited Elliot terminus of B By 175th R.F.A. also horse lines of 101st L.F.B. Elliot of new Central Dump - reported to C.R.E. number of huts in LEPINETTE & Bac Nouveau were without water for artificial ventilation.	OK
CROIX DU BAC	15.iii.16	11½a	Rode ARMENTIERES r/inspected area occupied by Staff at R.E. Dump, 209 Coy Horselines R.E. Camp, r/Billets occupied by C Coy, 21st Northumberland Fusiliers, & in afternoon r/visited Billets occupied by 20th Northumberland Fusiliers & HQrs of 20th R.F., & 102nd Bde HQn — arranging for clearing out of Brown Kitchen Pt.	OK

WAR DIARY or INTELLIGENCE SUMMARY

Army Form C. 2118.

Place	Date	Hour	Summary of Events and Information	Remarks and references to Appendices
CROIX DU BAC	16.iii.16	11 h⁻	Rode RUE DELATREE Trenches & Camps. Billet occupied by 25th Northumberland Fusiliers recently vacated by 15th Royal Scots not satisfactory. Arrangements (for sterilizing utensils (for washing utensils), & the disposal of refuse. On to ERQUINGHEM. Trenches (for fatigue parties) to clear up River Bellot in CHAPELLE ARMENTIERES. Visited BAC ST MAUR Trenches & YMCA Hut Latrines & urinals, area which was in an unsatisfactory condition — reported same.	O/C
CROIX DU BAC	17.iii.16	11 h⁻	Rode to STEENWERCKE with officer from Rest Camp. Site occupied by Bombing School. Discussed various sanitary arrangements. Water supply. In afternoon rode to L'EPINETTE with officer. Thus visited new Rested troops & refuse. Rode STEENWERCKE. Saw civilian, called a possible victim of trench fever in front of LITTLE PAQUOT.	O/C
CROIX DU BAC	18.iii.16	11 h⁻	Rode to RUE MARLE & CHAPELLE ARMENTIERES Interviewed Staff Captain of 102nd Infy Bde & arranged for hurdles and/or incinerator collar releasing Cellar on ARMENTIERES papers (for Vidors). A.S.C. Transport (for emptying of cesspit - paid civilians & sanitary contractor at ERQUINGHEM & gen. order in for sanitary work. Rode to ESTAIRES with officer. & was present at discussion on Trench Fever etc.	O/C
CROIX DU BAC	19.iii.16	7.30 h⁻	Visited Central Incinerator at L'EPINETTE (Interview) Officers of 15th Royal Scots on army discussed report. Manure on marsh from H.Q. stables. Visit Camp of D4, & H.T. Transport. In afternoon - visit Field Ambulance at BAILLEUL (Hill House) 26th Field Ambulance that at CROIX DU BAC. Child not seen. And Batts at Royal (Hill House).	O/C

2353 Wt. W2544/1454 700,000 5/15 D. D. & L. A.D.S.S./Forms/C. 2118.

WAR DIARY
or
INTELLIGENCE SUMMARY
(Erase heading not required.)

Army Form C. 2118.

Place	Date	Hour	Summary of Events and Information	Remarks and references to Appendices
CROIX DU BAC	20.iii.16	11 pm	Rode L'EPINETTE, RUE MARLE, CHAPELLE ARMENTIERES, GRIS POT, L'ARMÉE & RUE DE LATRÉE. Inspected various camps, billets, latrines & various sanitary arrangements.	W.
CROIX DU BAC	21.iii.16	11 pm	Rode BAC ST MAUR, Paraded for various sanitary improvements in areas occupied by 97th of 2nd R.B. Ambulance & A.D.M.S. 34th Div - also in (CROIX DU BAC - In afternoon rode to L'EPINETTE & ERQUINGHEM visited various billets, camps, improvements, latrines & new toilet incinerator.	W.
CROIX DU BAC	22.iii.16	11.30 pm	Rode BAC ST MAUR, ERQUINGHEM, RUE MARLE, CHAPELLE ARMENTIERES inspected various billets, farms, bivouacs, latrines in improvements. Interviewed Mayor of CHAPELLE ARMENTIÈRES.	W.
CROIX DU BAC	23.iii.16	11 pm	Went FLEURBAIX & inspected out billets, tents &c occupied the same evening by 101st Brigade (Infantry) comprising 4 Battalions by 1st Hants & 1 Sussex Battalion of 29th Division. While afternoon to RUE MARLE & various arrangements for dinner &c at Fort Hotel advance Headquarters of 178th Bgde RFA	W.
CROIX DU BAC	24.iii.16	11 pm	Visited various billets turned (CROIX DU BAC, BAC ST MAUR & FORT ROMPU Farms &c) for sanitary improvements.	W.
CROIX DU BAC	25.iii.16	7 pm	Rode BAC ST MAUR, ERQUINGHEM, ROLANDERIE, RUE DE LATRÉE & FLEURBAIX. Inspected various camps, billets &c - various of 36th Division & Corps Troops. Arranged for various sanitary measures.	W.
CROIX DU BAC	26.iii.16	10.30 pm	Rode L'EPINETTE inspected billets of 83 Bgde 175th RFA also Corps Divisional Incinerator, Inspected ERQUINGHEM Hop of schulete. Made various arrangements for work of subordinate officer. Sanitary.	W.

WAR DIARY
or
INTELLIGENCE SUMMARY.

Army Form C. 2118.

Place	Date	Hour	Summary of Events and Information	Remarks and references to Appendices
			Section. In afternoon inspected new Camp of Bombing School near CROIX DU BAC.	OR
CROIX DU BAC	27.iii.16	11 pm	Rode BAILLEUL for L'ERQUINGHEM, had interview with CROIX DU BAC & to RUE MARLE, near Brigadier General regards supply of experts in afternoon took new bath outside billet of 176th RFA Bgde; also inspected billet of B Batty 20 brigade Rudders into STEENWERCK had interview.	OR
CROIX DU BAC	28.iii.16	11 pm	Rode BAILLEUL, Hurland Hatt for classify stature. In afternoon at L'EPINETTE inspected Conducted recreation & Well inspected (Batt) 175th RFA to ARMENTIERES much improvement in supply of experts in RUE MARLE & Rudders - rode BAC ST MAUR farm w/ with APM [illegible] photos of pillbox to draw stature month.	OR
CROIX DU BAC	29.iii.16	11 pm	Rode FLEURBAIX in morn (1) visited various billets of 10th Brigade (Infantry) regarding [illegible] of ditches. In afternoon took STEENWERCK [illegible] with 8th Division Sanitary officer up the Division Farms pit for horses of STEENWERCK and 17th Division on April 15-16. On to ERQUINGHEM & saw Staff Supt. then down to HQ quartermaster.	OR
CROIX DU BAC	30.iii.16	11 pm	Rode ERQUINGHEM inspected [illegible] 160th Bd RFA station for ARMENTIERES inspected RE dump. In afternoon rode to FLEURBAIX inspected various billets of 10th Rudders in 16th North W Funston.	OR

WAR DIARY
or
INTELLIGENCE SUMMARY.

(Erase heading not required.)

Army Form C. 2118.

Place	Date	Hour	Summary of Events and Information	Remarks and references to Appendices
CROIX DU BAC	31.iii.16	11 p.m.	Recce BAILLEUL to HAZEBROUCK for Infantry/Transport on FARMENTIERS road for Empty - if ought at RUE MARLE to STEENWERCK road cartier lanterns - visited Asst Cyclist 2nd CROIX DU BAC - returned esta. for Motor cc. - Motor-cycle orderlies taken to the station.	a/c.
				A Stewart Capt E Police C.I.

74 San Sec
Vol 4
34th Div

War Diary

of

O/c 74th Sanitary Section
34th Division

April 1916.

Vol. No 4

WAR DIARY or INTELLIGENCE SUMMARY.

Army Form C. 2118.

Instructions regarding War Diaries and Intelligence Summaries are contained in F. S. Regs., Part II. and the Staff Manual respectively. Title pages will be prepared in manuscript.

(Erase heading not required.)

Place	Date	Hour	Summary of Events and Information	Remarks and references to Appendices
CROIX DU BAC	1.IV.16	11 pm	R.tc L'ESTRADE - nightly rest camp of 102nd Field Ambulance, yesterday visited and selected reinforcements. Conducted reconnaissance at L'EPINETTE. To ERQUINGHEM - had conference via field Ambulance offices. Found the villages arranging for clearing out of patients. Pass civilians at CROIX DU BAC.	W.D.
CROIX DU BAC	2.IV.16	11 pm	Visit various areas around ERQUINGHEM. Camps recently vacated by 15th Royal Scots at Rest Camp were L'EPINETTE - Visit Hostile occupied by 20th R.B. Northumberland Fusiliers.	W.D.
CROIX DU BAC	3.IV.16	11 pm	Sent fatigue party to clean up Camps recently vacated by 15th Royal Scots. M.H.s 1st southern in/c ERQUINGHEM and Camps. Notified W.O.T to arrange next reports by 16th Royal Scots + 11th Suffolks at FORT ROM PU + 4,209th C.R.E. at ERQUINGHEM. Individual work parties for future hospital for BAC ST MAUR + the future party for APM 36th Division. Sanitary Officer of 2nd Australian Division + Brain camps for in shortage of parties.	W.D.
CROIX DU BAC	4.IV.16	11 pm	Visit STEENWERCKE, ARMENTIERES, CHAPELLE ARMENTIERES, RUE MARLE, L'HALLOBEAU, FORT ROM PU + FLEURBAIX with D. San Sec of 2nd Australian Division, including various Camps + trenches.	W.D.
CROIX DU BAC	5.IV.16	11 pm	Include fatigue 206th (6)1 R.E. at RUE MARLE; Visit 102nd F.A. at STEENWERCKE. Inspected Hos pital Billet. Include Camps lately vacated by 15th Royal Scots at L'HALLOBEAU + ensured work by fatigue party. Camps were at first time occupied by Infantry of 2nd Australian Division.	W.D.

Army Form C. 2118.

WAR DIARY
or
INTELLIGENCE SUMMARY.
(Erase heading not required.)

Instructions regarding War Diaries and Intelligence Summaries are contained in F.S. Regs., Part II. and the Staff Manual respectively. Title pages will be prepared in manuscript.

Place	Date	Hour	Summary of Events and Information	Remarks and references to Appendices
CROIX DU BAC	6.IV.16	7.30pm	Rd. ARMENTIERES paraway for supplies (Cruplet at RUE MARLE on to CHAPELLE ARMENTIERES PRUE MARLE thro' steady rain. Billets paraway for three brigade (extra very vacated) — on to ERQUINGHEM refugee camp fit (empty by Australian Division) BAT	DR
CROIX DU BAC	7.IV.16	11pm	Rd. BAILLEUL for cash on to L'EPINETTE — ERQUINGHEM in billets British at Turcoing — Menin Camp, Thilute Turcoing area and ERQUINGHEM. In afternoon visited Armand Drouin (Water Works Australian) at CHAPELLE ARMENTIERES & various billets in RUE MARLE.	DR
CROIX DU BAC	8.IV.16	11pm	Rd. RUE MARLE thro' steady natural Paral(?)trial which has occurred in 16th Battalion pavilion — on ARMENTIERES. Paid for laundry & supplies at RUE MARLE.	DR
			Had various arrangements for leave here as in 10.IV.16.	
CROIX DU BACQ	9.IV.16	11pm	Attended Sanitary meeting of Divisional officers with Captain BYRNE O.C. of Sanitary Section of 2nd Australian Division — visited Bouhy School (used into Captain BYRNE)	DR
TILQUES	10.IV.16	8.45pm	Move with Section to TILQUES.	DR
TILQUES	11.IV.16	10.30pm	Tests water supplies in TILQUES & Carried out various sanitary arrangements in regard to billeting of billets for incoming troops.	DR

2353 Wt. W2514/1454 700,000 5/15 D.D.&L. A.D.S.S./Forms/C. 2118.

Army Form C. 2118.

WAR DIARY
or
INTELLIGENCE SUMMARY.
(Erase heading not required.)

Place	Date	Hour	Summary of Events and Information	Remarks and references to Appendices
TILQUES	12.IV.16	11 p.a.	Visited various billets in & around TILQUES (various) for sanitary improvement. In afternoon went to ST OMER for materials. Sent six members of Section to LUMBRES & then attached to detach't of 104th Fld Ambulance for sanitary duties in surrounding areas.	ADS
TILQUES	13.IV.16	10 p.a.	Visited billets in & around TILQUES in morning — in afternoon went to SETQUES, LUMBRES & AFFRINGUES where 152nd Bde RFA, 160th Bde RFA, 175th Bde RFA had respective quarters — also visited detachment of 104th Fld at LUMBRES. Saw 15th Royal Scots at TATINGHEM where they had just arrived from Stages, one night.	ADS
TILQUES	14.IV.16	11 p.a.	Rode to EPERLECQUES & HELLEBROUCQ to see 15th Royal Scots, who had just arrived at the former place, & 102nd Fld Ambulance at the latter — on to HOULLE where 18th Royal Scots had just arrived. In afternoon rode to NORDAUSQUES & RECQUES to arrange water under of 10th & 11th Fd Bdes. Also saw of 11th Scott Greys who were [former] place.	ADS
TILQUES	15.IV.16	7.30 p.a.	Rode ZUDAUSQUES & BOISDINGHEM — [visited] 25th Northumberland Fusiliers at the former place — on to BOISDINGHEM & returned H.Q. of 18th Northumberland Fusiliers regarding [sanitary?] arrangements for Battalion. In afternoon made various arrangements regarding [return?] to TILQUES.	ADS
TILQUES	16.IV.16	7 p.hr	Rode WATTEN interviewed Mayor [arrange] for supply of fresh water from town supply for troops in neighbourhood.	ADS

WAR DIARY
or
INTELLIGENCE SUMMARY.

(Erase heading not required.)

Army Form C. 2118.

Place	Date	Hour	Summary of Events and Information	Remarks and references to Appendices
TILQUES	17.IV.16	10 /n	Rode NORDAUSQUES & NORTLEULINGHEM - investigated arrangements for baths by 21st & 22nd North'umberland Fusiliers. One of WESTROVE & investigated same arrangements made by 23rd R.F.s - visited 16th Royal Scots at HOULLE regarding same matter.	OMS
TILQUES	18.IV.16	10 /n	Rode HOULLE, EPERLECQUES & OUEST MONT - selected sites for shower baths, sent for number of 74th Sanitary Section - rigged baths at HOULLE, EPERLECQUES for 16th & 15th Royal Scots respectively - arranged for baths to be erected on plans, 3 day, for 10th Durhams at OUEST MONT.	OMS
TILQUES	19.IV.16	7 pm	Sent Disinfector (Steam) EPERLECQUES to disinfect various clothing of 15th Royal Scots, also to number of 15th Suffolks. Erected shower baths for 10th Durhams at OUEST MONT — 15 afterwards arrived at same. MS. Rode NORTBECOURT selected site for shower bath for 11th Suffolks. 15 afterwards arrived.	OMS
TILQUES	20.IV.16	10 /n	Rode LUMBRES, AFFRINGUES & COULEMBY — saw MOs of 160-175th R.F.A & D.A.C. respectively re various Sanitary arrangements — sort out fragments & mis-structures for construction of proposed latrines to all MOs & OCs of Field Ambulances in Division.	OMS
TILQUES	21.IV.16	7 /n	Visited various billets at TILQUES & arranged for certain Sanitary improvements — In afternoon to MORINGHEM and visited billets occupied by 207 & 6? R.C. fusils. Sanitary conditions very bad — told water from their watercart (found it unchlorinated) — reported conditions to A.D.M.S.	OMS

WAR DIARY or INTELLIGENCE SUMMARY.

(Erase heading not required.)

Army Form C. 2118.

5

Place	Date	Hour	Summary of Events and Information	Remarks and references to Appendices
TILQUES	22.IV.16	7pm	MOULLE - Visited billets occupied by 24th C.F.F. Reconnd water for watering cattle found only satisfactory with exception of some fauces unturned overflowing troughs & tanks for latrines.	OR
TILQUES	22.IV.16		Rode NORDAUSQUES RECQUES MOULLE - Interviewed O.Cs of 21st, 20th 24th C.F.F. Infantry - Selected sites for portable show baths for 21st C.F.F. - Rode ST OMER & attained sawdust & Kerosene tins for latrines. Sent Hitchcock to 25th C.F.F. & 160th R.F.A. at LUMBRES about same. Arranged with Hitchcock send Various stores under.	OR
TILQUES	23.IV.16	7pm	Rode ST OMER & obtained sawdust & number of kerosene drums for use as latrines, incinerator Various billets around TILQUES. In afternoon rode LUMBRES & interviewed Staff/Sgt Hitchcock i/c Sub-Section of 74th San Sec about various arrangements, inspected billets occupied by O.C. & O.Cs. of 160th R.F.A. - Interviewed M.O. of 152nd R.F.A. at SETQUES.	OR
TILQUES	24.IV.16	10pm	Inspected billets of 25th Northumberland Fusiliers at ZOUDAUSQUES & in afternoon rode to NORTLEULINGHEM & inspected billets occupied by 22nd Northumberland Fusiliers proceeded to EPERLECQUES & inspected billets occupied by throughout	OR
TILQUES	25.IV.16	10pm	Rode RECQUES & inspected billets occupied by 20th Northumberland Fusiliers, Veterinary	OR

Place	Date	Hour	Summary of Events and Information	Remarks and references to Appendices
			In O.I. afternoon visit to BERGUES and visit to Billets received by 28th Northumberland Fusiliers, Fort WATTEN & HELLEBROUCQ. Made arrangements for sanitation of latter place. Previous clothing with O.C. 102nd Field Ambulance at latter place.	MT CBT.
TILQUES	26.IV.16	12.30p	Visited various billets at TILQUES. Made arrangements for Sanitary work to be done during my absence on leave. Went on leave until 4.V.16.	

B. Bronde Capt. R.A.M.C.

WAR DIARY

of

7th Sanitary Section.

May 1916

Vol 5

Army Form C. 2118.

WAR DIARY
or
INTELLIGENCE SUMMARY.
(Erase heading not required.)

Instructions regarding War Diaries and Intelligence Summaries are contained in F.S. Regs., Part II. and the Staff Manual respectively. Title pages will be prepared in manuscript.

Place	Date	Hour	Summary of Events and Information	Remarks and references to Appendices
TILQUES	5.V.16	10 p.m.	Arrived TILQUES from Scarr 11.30 p.m. 4.V.16. Rode ST OMER in morning & reported to Major LOCK on MOULLE, HOULLE & OUEST MONT inspected various billets resulting vacated by 24th Northumberland Fusiliers, 16th Royal Scots & 10th Lincolns - collected some ammunition equipment left by troops. - In afternoon rode to ZOUDAUSQUES & inspected billets resulting vacated by 25th Northumberland Fusiliers.	O.R.
BRESLE	6.V.16	11.30 p.m.	Sent member of 74th Sanitary Section by rail from STOMER to LONGUEAU. He motorlorry proceeded by road to BRESLE, rode by motor cycle to BRESLE arrived 9.30 p.m. Before leaving wrote note to NORTLEULINGHEM, NORDAUSQUES, RECQUES & inspected billets resulting vacated by 22nd, 21st, & 20th Northumberland Fusiliers.	O.R.
BRESLE	7.V.16	10 p.m.	Reported to ADMS of Division at HQn at BAIZIEUX, visited various billets in BRESLE & arranged Sanitary work for men in the village.	O.R.
BRESLE	8.V.16	10 p.m.	Reported to ADMS at HQn (Div) & arranged for entire Sanitary work of the 8th Div - continued Sanitary work in BRESLE. Rode BEHENCOURT & selected billets for 74th Sanitary Section.	O.R.
BEHENCOURT	9.V.16	10 p.m.	Moved to BEHENCOURT & inspected various billets in village.	O.R.
BEHENCOURT	10.V.16	Morning	Inspected some quarters of Sanitary Section & area occupied by troops, at & near BEHENCOURT. Carried out various Sanitary improvements & rode to BAISIEUX & saw A.D.M.S.	O.R.

2353 Wt. W2544/1454 700,000 5/15 D D. & L. A.D.S.S./Forms/C. 2118.

WAR DIARY or INTELLIGENCE SUMMARY

Army Form C. 2118.

(Erase heading not required.)

Place	Date	Hour	Summary of Events and Information	Remarks and references to Appendices
BEHENCOURT	10.VII.16	10.30 p.m.	Mr W BRESLE & Lt ITMAN of Sanitary Section of VIIIth Division at HENENCOURT.	ADP
BEHENCOURT	11.VII.16	10.30 p.m.	Sent member of Sanitary Section to FRANVILLERS, BRESLE & other villages near BEHENCOURT to arrange sanitary improvements & water supplies. Rode to FRANVILLERS, BRESLE & DERNAN-COURT. Visited Town Major in their places arranging for sanitary work for new units of Sanitary Section who posted at their places. In afternoon I had W/Sir F HENENCOURT. Interviewed O.C. Sanitary Section of VIIIth Division & discussed various Sanitary arrangements that might be necessary on to moving day of the two divisions. Visited various Camps with him.	ADP
BEHENCOURT	12.VII.16	7 pm	Sent two members of the VIIIth Sanitary Section for duties in Sanitary Inspection in each of the following places:- FRANVILLERS, LA HOUSSOYE, BRESLE, DERNANCOURT, not BEAUCOURT & interviewed Field Cashier. In afternoon rode BAISIEUX & HENENCOURT. Could not procure Sanitary work in BEHENCOURT.	ADP
BEHENCOURT	13.VII.16	11 pm	Rode ALBERT via (various) Town Major regarding posting of a number of Sanitary to town in their on Plumer(?) day - Visited various billets occupied by Maj 176 R.F.A., 103rd B.P. & Machine Gunners, & Marched of 10 ext Field Ambulance - Called at BASIEUX & reported to A.D.M.S. on return journey.	ADP
BEHENCOURT	14.VII.16	11 am	Rode DERNANCOURT via A.O. of 176 - B.G. R.F.A. regarding his lines, interviewed Asst. of W.C.R.E. Fauquier regarding various matters, also Town Major & had of 21st Northumberland Fusiliers, rode on to ALBERT. Then...	ADP

Army Form C. 2118.

WAR DIARY
or
INTELLIGENCE SUMMARY.
(Erase heading not required.)

Instructions regarding War Diaries and Intelligence Summaries are contained in F. S. Regs., Part II. and the Staff Manual respectively. Title pages will be prepared in manuscript.

Place	Date	Hour	Summary of Events and Information	Remarks and references to Appendices
BEHENCOURT	14.V.16		Sanitary Officer of VIII Division in district (Battn. concentration Z) in ALBERT — visited various areas with Serjeant of 74th Sanitary Section running all sanitary work. — Returning O.C. 15th Shott ambulance Pavilion. — Reported to ADMS at BAIZIEUX. That arrangements for Battn. ALBERT return of officer.	O.R. O.R.
BEHENCOURT	15.V.16	11 hr	Rode ALBERT met Colonel SHAKESPEARE, O.C. 15th ? Battn. — Discussed incident & visited Battn. accepted by 2nd & 126th Institutions Pavilion. — Saw M.O. 15th Shott. & R. + discussed various sanitary arrangements.	
BEHENCOURT	16.V.16	11 hr	Rode LA HOUSSOYE & saw Town Major re-visited certain billets with him Remained sanitary matters. In afternoon rode to BAIZIEUX visited D.A.D.M.S. — on to DERNANCOURT saw M.O. of 27th Shott ambulance Pavilion (at PARK) visited camps occupied by troops attached to 34th Division at DERNANCOURT re sanitary for certain requirements. Interviewed Adjutant of C.R.E. made timber for latrines.	O.R.
BEHENCOURT	17.V.16	11 hr	Rode FRANVILLERS enquired re show Battn. — on to DERNANCOURT met Corporal in charge of army of 74th Sanitary Section and to best billet, visited various billets & camps. Remained in afternoon visited ALBERT in district, latrines & certain other billets. Selected a site for erection of incinerator there return from French.	O.R.
BEHENCOURT	18.V.16	11 hr	Rode BAISSIEUX reported to ADMS — arranged for Union, out of infantry Yard at H.Qr. Return improvements. On to BRESLE re Town Major arrangements for drum, out of billets in.	

2353 Wt. W2544/1454 700,000 5/15 D. D. & L. A.D.S.S./Forms/C. 2118.

WAR DIARY
or
INTELLIGENCE SUMMARY

Army Form C. 2118.

Place	Date	Hour	Summary of Events and Information	Remarks and references to Appendices
			out and of village — Saw Staff Captain of 101st Bde. reerranged for later a party of 200 men for this morning following — Visited a number of billets occupied by 15th & 16th Royal Scots — interviewed their M.O. re sanitary & various improvements. Night HQrs again in error & see program.	M.R.
BEHENCOURT	19.VII.16	10.0 a.m.	Inspected FRANVILLERS & DERNANCOURT in turn — Town Major — found a number of insanitary conditions reported same to ADMS. Requested Town Major — Called BRESLE in evening & see program re returning Staff Captain of 101st Brigade.	M.R.
BEHENCOURT	20.VII.16	11 a.m.	Called BAIZIEUX reported to ADMS — advised in turn & manner at HQrs (Div) proceeded to BRESLE & DERNANCOURT — visited various billets — on to ALBERT reerranged for erection of showerbath in RUE DE NEMOURS.	M.R.
BEHENCOURT	21.VII.16	11 p.m.	Visited 2 huts on site of AMIENS — ALBERT road & found these in unsatisfactory condition — visited well near ALBERT situated Eg Central ALBERT Command Shirt — On to MEAULTE & visited 105th F.A., 1727 R.G.A. Heavy Battery — On to ALBERT visited billets & provided site for horses & have ten men with Town Major — inspected various billets in ALBERT.	M.R.
BEHENCOURT	22.VII.16	11 p.m.	Arranged for cleaning huts on ALBERT roadside — visited HQrs (Div), on to BRESLE — interviewed R.O. of 24th North Staffs — inspected showers & hutments — inspected Horse Lines of 1st cohort (104th) 11th Suffolks, 175th Royal Scots — on to DERNANCOURT visited a number of billets re sanitary for Sanitary improvements. Reported to ADMS at BAIZIEUX.	M.R.

WAR DIARY
or
INTELLIGENCE SUMMARY.
(Erase heading not required.)

Army Form C. 2118.

Place	Date	Hour	Summary of Events and Information	Remarks and references to Appendices
BEHENCOURT	23.II.16	11 a	Rode DERNANCOURT met DADMS visited a number of Albert units here. Tested water in well situated E of (ALBERT Cemetery Chisel?) - Inspected Trenches occupied by 15th Royal Scots. Rifles. Disinfector treated 750 blankets.	A.T.
BEHENCOURT	24.II.16	11 a.m.	Brickfields blankets & clothes, at BEHENCOURT inspected. Bathing arrangements with Town Major — Visited BAISIEUX trained A.D.M.S. Disinfector blankets.	A.T.
BEHENCOURT	25.II.16	11.15 a	Visited FRANVILLERS inspected work - saw Staff Captain of 102nd Inf'y Bde regarding removal of manure from buildings — passed to ALBERT inspected Division of Branch for repair of man. Disinfector reports, return of inoculation - inspected various billets occupied by 16th Royal Scots r. 1017 Coy. Machine Guns. Disinfector 1050 blankets.	A.T.
BEHENCOURT	26.II.16	11.15 a	Rode BAIZIEUX inspected A.D.M.S. on to BRESLE & inspected certain sanitary work - To ALBERT inspected various area medical arrangements for sanitary improvements - on to DERNANCOURT met DADMS & inspected number of billets & insanitary areas.	O.R.
BEHENCOURT	Feb. 8.1916	11 a.m.	Rode BRESLE inspected camps billets of 22nd, 25th, 26th, 27th Northumberland Fusiliers, also Brig'y Train - In afternoon inspected billets occupied by 152nd Bde R.F.A. at BEHENCOURT. Paid men.	O.R.
BEHENCOURT	26.II.16	11 a.m.	Rode RIBEMONT inspected camps, transport by 1, 2, 3, Coy of S.C. on to ALBERT visited camps of Diva on way made arrangements with Town Major for utter sanitary disposal in filthy insanitary areas back to the billets.	O.R.

WAR DIARY
or
INTELLIGENCE SUMMARY.
(Erase heading not required.)

Army Form C. 2118.

Place	Date	Hour	Summary of Events and Information	Remarks and references to Appendices
BEHENCOURT	29.V.16	11 a.m.	Visited BAISIEUX, ALBERT, BRESLE & DERNANCOURT with Sanitary Officer of 4th Army — Major LOWE, & DADMS of 34th Division (Major BURKE), in afternoon m[o]t[ore]d to ALBERT & inspected the divisional incinerator. Made arrangements for [?] with Dr. Don in reserve, but [?]	OR
BEHENCOURT	30.V.16	10.30 a.m.	Rode BAIZIEUX m[otore]d to DADMS, on to BRESLE m[otore]d to work on A.D.M.S. ALBERT. Saw Town Major. Made arrangements to repair [latrine?] position, visited 101st Fd B[earer] T[rain]? w/o BELLE VUE Farm. Arranged for loan of films in return for Cubicles, [?] for Dr. [?] children in dugout near USNA REDOUBT m[otore]d to ALBERT m[otore]d to work at West end of ALBERT. [?] incinerator [?] by [?] party	OR
BEHENCOURT	31.V.16	10.30 a.m.	Rode DERNANCOURT visited various billets. Though in distinct[?] arrang[ed] for Sanitary work there by Sub-section of 34th Sanitary Section in that village.	OR

(?) Brown Capt. RAMC

"4 Sanbre Vol 6
June

Sqd 2nd
June 1916

WAR-DIARY

of

O/C 7Ath. SANITARY. SECTION
34^h. DIVISION

JUNE - 1916.

PAGES. 7

VOL. 6.

WAR DIARY
or
INTELLIGENCE SUMMARY.

(Erase heading not required.)

Army Form C 2118.

Place	Date	Hour	Summary of Events and Information	Remarks and references to Appendices
BEHENCOURT	1.vi.16	11 pm	Visits paid by C Battery 152nd Bde RFA at BEHENCOURT where card to be visited by Lieut. was visited. Tonnage for physical + internal acct Tonnage. Rode BAIZIEUX + reported ADMS. at 2 Divisional Bomb. School Tonnage for Sanitary work in Camp. Rode on to ALBERT. Thirty-third incinerator in use. Was of room - Saw Town Major. Then at 16th Royal Scots & 178th Bde RFA. Talked with latter to DERIVANCOURT – reported his repair of their major Tonnage in Sanitary improvements.	O.R.
BEHENCOURT	11.vi.16	11 pm	Rode LA HOUSSOYE, FRANVILLARS & BRESLE inspected Camps, Billets, interviewing Town Majors The O.C. Tonnage for Sanitary improvements.	C.M.S.
BEHENCOURT	111.vi.16	10 am	Rode DERNANCOURT met DADMS inspecting various parts of village, made certain arrangements with reverr. A.C.O (Sani. Sup) in charge. Rode on to BRAY. Visit O.C. 30th Divisional Sani. Sec. Then review Sanitary contrivances. Called at ALBERT ISAC's mess A.C.O in charge making arrangements for work. Passed to FRANVILLERS reached at 102nd Fuld Ambulance & made further arrangements with Town Major.	O.R.
BEHENCOURT	11.vi.16	pm	Rode FRANVILLERS inspected Market on ALBERT & interviewed member of San. Section, stating inten- tion of DERNANCOURT & then continue.— To HEILLY Saw— MAJOR THOMPSON O.C. Casualty Clearing Station. Made Sergt White wished in found his eye while on Sanitary duties at ALBERT – on to BRESLE, Saw Inventor of Sanitary Stoves. On to BAIZIEUX reported to ADMS.	O.R.

WAR DIARY
INTELLIGENCE SUMMARY

Army Form C. 2118.

Place	Date	Hour	Summary of Events and Information	Remarks and references to Appendices
BEHENCOURT	5.VI.16	10.30 a.m.	Boys captured (from patrols reports) on MONTIGNY – BEAUCOURT road – communicated with Town Mayor at BEHENCOURT re visit at P.M. of British Patrol and estates proceedings which were carried out – Inspected number of French in BEHENCOURT which was a war camp which caused trouble of officers, to reports to Town Major. Rode ALBERT in afternoon re sister camp of DAC & other service on way – interviewed Senior N.C.O. & Sanitary Section at ALBERT.	ADS
BEHENCOURT	6.VI.16	10 a.m.	Inspected various billets in BEHENCOURT – Rode FRANVILLERS in afternoon & inspected billets there. Senior N.C.O. stated there on BAIZIEUX reported to ADMS.	ADS
BEHENCOURT	7.VI.16	10 a.m.	Rode DERNANCOURT re visited a number of billets – on to ALBERT re visited there. In an interview with billets made arrangements for cleaning, fresh paint & water closets in permanent.	ADS
BEHENCOURT	8.VI.16	10 a.m.	Rode BAIZIEUX re ported at ADMS Office – arrangements for work at but then re visited Bombing School (British) & inspected recent Sanitary work. – on to ALBERT re visited 23rd Northumberland Fusiliers & travellers stationed Medical Officer.	ADS
BEHENCOURT	9.VI.16	10 a.m.	Rode FRANVILLERS re visited various billets – met Lt Colonel IRVINE O/c 102nd Field Ambulance discussed various Sanitary matters – on to BRESLE re visited billets occupied by 101st Inf. Bde, on to DERNANCOURT.	ADS
BEHENCOURT	10.VI.16	9 a.m.	Inspected trenches occupied by 22nd Northumb'd – In afternoon rode ALBERT & DERNANCOURT re inspected Temporary hospitals, 14 in number, who were on fatigue (Sanitary) under Reported ADMS.	ADS

Army Form C. 2118.

WAR DIARY
or
INTELLIGENCE SUMMARY.
(Erase heading not required.)

Instructions regarding War Diaries and Intelligence Summaries are contained in F. S. Regs., Part II. and the Staff Manual respectively. Title pages will be prepared in manuscript.

Place	Date	Hour	Summary of Events and Information	Remarks and references to Appendices
BEHENCOURT	11.vii.16	9.30 p.m	Rode FRANVILLERS, LAHOUSSOYE & BRESLE in spect. billets travaux [?] Sanitary work — on to FRECHENCOURT & Officers' mess for tiffin for District ports.	W.
BEHENCOURT	12.vii.16	11.30 p.m	Rode FRANVILLERS & visited various billets & 21st & 125th Northumberland Fusiliers — Inspected travaux water hauts — on ALBERT - AMIENS road — on to MOULIN du VIVIER visited camp of 125 R.G.A. & 52nd R.F.A. on to MEAULT — made appointment with No. of 23rd B. R.G.A. for Phone, Orgy — visited ALBERT new Search & C.O. of Sand. Section.	W.
BEHENCOURT	13.vii.16	11 p.m	Rode MEAULT - visited Q.D. of 23rd H.Q.A. R.G.A. Discussed Sanitary matters. Discussed camp occupied by 125th H.Q.A. — rode on to ALBERT met DADMS & D. Division. Discussed French occupied by 20 Searchlight Fusiliers...	W.
BEHENCOURT	14.vii.16	11.30 p.m	... arranged for scheme of sterilization of water in & Sellier Patrol train for Transport by lorries. Rode DERNANCOURT met DADMS of 34 Division. Discussed various manner of billets & camp.	W.
BEHENCOURT	15.vii.16	11 p.m	Rode FRANVILLERS travaux, insp for Latrines auts, &c. Traveled clothes for baths bad. French on ALBERT - AMIENS road — on & ALBERT visited DERNANCOURT — on & MOULIN DU VIVIER Travaux of various incendiary Latrines.	W.
BEHENCOURT	16.vii.16	9.30 p.m	Rode FRECHENCOURT & various T.V. area on fatigue duty — on & FRANVILLERS & inspected construction of Latrines for guard on waterhead — on & MOULIN DU VIVIER inspected Sanitary arrangements & construction for Incinerators (H.Qrs Staff) — to ALBERT & visited pumps (Water Manufactory pumps) Station &c.	W.

Army Form C. 2118.

WAR DIARY
or
INTELLIGENCE SUMMARY.
(Erase heading not required.)

Instructions regarding War Diaries and Intelligence Summaries are contained in F. S. Regs., Part II. and the Staff Manual respectively. Title pages will be prepared in manuscript.

Place	Date	Hour	Summary of Events and Information	Remarks and references to Appendices
BEHENCOURT	17.VI.16	11 p.m	Investigated source of water supply in BEHENCOURT from stream - made certain arrangements for drawing river supply. Filtrates - also inspected tanks of [illegible] up & spring near BEAUCOURT - returned. Captain KIDD O/C 21st C.F.R.C. regards provision of latrines for draft 12 at pumping stations also - also must arrangements for proper latrine accommodation for 81st Ref RFet off 14th Division. To forward full states of water. Rode MOULIN DU VIVIER - visited Sanitary arrangement for Divl HQrs Bayeux - on to ALBERT - saw Town Major regards various matters, re DERNANCOURT. Saw A.C.O. in charge & interview & Baizieux re pont & A.D.M.S.	A/c
BEHENCOURT	18.VI.16	11.30 p.m	Inspected water situation at BEHENCOURT for storage - to FRANVILLERS - returned views A.C.O. at DERNANCOURT - arranged sanitary work - St ALBERT - visited Traders - arranged for latrine etc and for advanced Dressing Stations - other matters - rode MOULIN DU VIVIER returned O.C. of 105th Field Ambulance calling DERNANCOURT on return. Survey Historical review A.C.O.	A/c
BEHENCOURT	19.VI.16	11 p.m	Rode ALBERT - visited Traders inspected work at advanced Dressing Station. Inspect Captain FIDDIAN Q.M.O. of 11th Suffolk. This braud sector of Trenches occupied by Fifth Brigade chronic sits for Regimental Aid Post. Reported to A.D.M.S.	A/c
BEHENCOURT	20.VI.16	11 p.m	Rode to ALBERT - visited advanced Dressing station at Site of NORTHUMBERLAND AVENUE - made further enquiries latter Sup. Visited DERNANCOURT - arranged for latrines, water supply &c & proper collection	

2353 Wt. W2544/1454 700,000 5/15 D. D. & L. A.D.S.S./Forms/C. 2118.

WAR DIARY
or
INTELLIGENCE SUMMARY.
(Erase heading not required.)

Army Form C. 2118.

Place	Date	Hour	Summary of Events and Information	Remarks and references to Appendices
BEHENCOURT	27th June		Station for wounded – Back to ALBERT principal work of fatigue parties. Saw ADMS re his instructions in reference to water tanks at upper end of BERKSHIRE AVENUE. Inspected water stand pipes & taps in town at BEHENCOURT. Found R.C.O. & in field stream & its ever Distribution – Rode DERNANCOURT – Findlat camp occupied by WORCESTER regiment reported number of insanitary conditions Etc.O. On ALBERT it is filled with of sanitary features at the H.Q. Northumberland Street – on latrines for advanced press stations – on to the top of BERKSHIRE AVENUE – instructed him to take latrines & urinals away – water found broken drains – returned & tanks emptied & matter sufficient in & Sanr Officer the H.Q water turned off to permit thoroughly wash out tanks in sewer. Reported to ADMS at H.Q.P. Saw R.C.O. & FRANVILLERS & inspected evacuating water supply, also DERNANCOURT. etc	☒
BEHENCOURT	28th June	11.30am	Rode BAIZIEUX – found ADMS out – went on to ALBERT that & found him. Talk of the / BERKSHIRE Avenue on H.Q.H. perfectly understood situation & saw that Cedars cultivators had run Carried but Matter – interviewed re future that the keep of arsenic had stopped and afterwards, and tanks – also stand in supply here before erosion found arsenic – Norfar concluded that arsenic was not to try with pillaging & tanks – On O'MODLIN DU VIVIER DERNANCOURT and if Cedar arrangements – on BAIZIEUX reported to ADMS. Saw Sanr R.C.O. & reported on all transfer appreciation & the situation in full & letter, Colonel GERRARD left to return as ADMS around DDMS to VIIIth Corps, Col. BLISS taking his place.	☒

2353 Wt. W2544/1454 700,000 5/15 D.D.&L. A.D.S.S./Forms/C. 2118.

Army Form C. 2118.

WAR DIARY
or
INTELLIGENCE SUMMARY.
(Erase heading not required.)

Place	Date	Hour	Summary of Events and Information	Remarks and references to Appendices
BEHENCOURT	23.VII.16	10 p	Rode BAIZIEUX reported to ADMS on to ALBERT & inspected water tank at top of BERKSHIRE AVENUE on to MOULIN DU VIVIERS PERNANCOURT removal of Institutes (Sanitary Section in from area.	CR
ALBERT	24.VII.16	10 p	Rode Institutes Sanitary Section. Saw O/c been 12 hours with Sergt FRANVILLERS (at Stables) 6/702 Fld Amb, 6/ MOULIN DU VIVIERS (at Stables) 10/34 F.A., 11/ ancient (ALBERT) (at Stables) 104 F.A. - The number of the 34th Sanitary Section was Walker for Police duties. Sanitary supervision - Statio/arms/ refuse disposal - control of transport arrangements (loading/unloading) - water testing etc., studying etc. - Clothing at Filththéodency m. Reported these with on ALBERT - Christ Sample Watertanks at top of BERKSHIRE Street in AVOCA VALLEY & sent these to 20/12 Mobile Hygiene Lab. at AMIENS for test for suicidal pollen. Inspected billets of 72/1st Army Troops R.E. from which carried out infected Enteric had been removed - found insanitary latrines	CR
ALBERT	25.VII.16	11/a	ALBERT shelled from 4.30 - 5.30 am - one 12 field st occupied by officers of 104 F.A. hit by shell Captain KELLY (firing halls) & 2nd BRISCOE wounded, 2nd HAWKSON missing wounded from which he evidently died on his way to Colean - Rode to 36 C.C.S. at HEILY to make arrangements for funeral, wanted from to BAIZIEUX (Divil HQn) reported to ADMS - had ALBERT & again visited tanks at top of BERKSHIRE AVENUE & took sample from stream to 20 F.A at EBART'S FARM for examination	CR

Army Form C. 2118.

WAR DIARY
or
INTELLIGENCE SUMMARY.
(Erase heading not required.)

Instructions regarding War Diaries and Intelligence Summaries are contained in F. S. Regs., Part II. and the Staff Manual respectively. Title pages will be prepared in manuscript.

Place	Date	Hour	Summary of Events and Information	Remarks and references to Appendices
ALBERT	26.VIII.16	10 p.m	Reported to ADMS at BAIZIEUX – inspected water supply at Div. HQn. Inspected camp of 11th Lt Inf.y Bn Staffs near BORE	A.R.
ALBERT	27.VIII.16	10 p.m	Held ADMS at MOULIN DU VIVIERS with OC's of 102nd, 103rd, 104th Field Ambulances, regarding arrangements for wounded, burial, conv.t. of structures. – RoR DERNANCOURT, BRESLE & FRANVILLERS. Interviewed Town Major – made arrangements for removal of inhabitants. Slept at ALBERT.	A.R.
ALBERT	28.VIII.16	10 p.m	Reported ADMS at BAIZIEUX – proceeded to ST GRATIEN & J.S.C. Made arrangement for Sanitary Corporal to be appointed to 2nd Field Coy R.S., to analyse water in tramways area in case of an advance. RoR DERNANCOURT (interview) C.R.E regarding attachment of Corporal ASHFORD 570q.t Coy R.E. – Proceeded to MOULIN DU VIVIERS & ADMS. Flat at H.Q. of Div'n. Hit arrangement where cancelled – Return to 100th F.A. Flat.y of quarters to HQn of Division.	A.R.
ALBERT	29.VIII.16	10 p.m	RoR BAIZIEUX reported to ADMS then went to MOULIN DU VIVIERS & ALBERT interviewing O.C. of 102nd, 103rd & 104th F.A. respectively – returned to BAIZIEUX & interviewed Senior P.C.O. of Sanitary made certain arrangements. DERNANCOURT interviews J Senior P.C.O.	A.R.
MOULIN DU VIVIER	30.VIII.16	10 p.m	Reported ADMS at BAIZIEUX returned to ALBERT. Proceeded to MOULIN DU VIVIER & returned Div.nal HQn visited 104th Field Ambulance Field B Lieut Brownhill	A.R.

(Sgd) Mitchell Capt R.A.M.C.
O.C. 74th Sanitary Section.

34th Divn.

Confidential.

War Diary

of

74th Sanitary Section

from July 1st 1916 to July 31st 1916.

(Volume 7)

COMMITTEE FOR THE
MEDICAL HISTORY OF THE WAR.
Date   31 AUG. 1916

July 1916

Army Form C. 2118.

WAR DIARY
or
INTELLIGENCE SUMMARY.
(Erase heading not required.)

Sheet No. 1

Place	Date	Hour	Summary of Events and Information	Remarks and references to Appendices
MOULIN DU VIVIER	1.VIII.16	10 p.m	Rode ALBERT reported O.C. 104th Field Ambulance & enquired in actively preparing — Rode BECOURT Chateau & visited afternoon Dressing Station (10th & 8th) & making certain sanitary arrangements with R.O. 1/c, also with Captain FIDDIAN, R.O. of 1st Suffolks, returning ALBERT returning 104th & drunk wounded.	WK
MOULIN DU VIVIER	2.VIII.16	10 p.m	Rode ALBERT returned O.C. 104th F.A. & handed over 1st Dressing Station in RUE D'AMIENS, for lightly wounded cases to O.C. 55th F.A. received other matters within 1st/H.D.W. with evacuation of Scottish treatment & transport of wounded. At 10 p.m. returned D.C. 104 & F.A. at MOULIN DUVIVIER for further of injuries hourly received from the mine air lift.	WK
MOULIN DU VIVIER	3.VIII.16	12 —	Went with ADMS to ALBERT meeting relieving O.C. 1/2nd F.A. making functions, D.R.S. – and DDMS (Col SKINNER) — ALBERT visited Advanced Station (10.2-7 p.m.) at DERNANCOURT — Rode BECOURT Chateau arrived 6.15 p.m. with party of 129 A.T. R.S.E. under 2 officers: stretcher wounded in 20 hours (and in park of Bgd). Was told [word] that they had all been visited — Returned ADMS.	OR
BAIZIEUX	4.VIII.16	10 p.m	Rode ALBERT & FRANVILLERS. Made arrangement for evacuation of Scottish Drawer Posts HqRS at BAIZIEUX — note forbid MOULIN DUVIVIER from BAIZIEU & mis, all route.	WK

Army Form C. 2118.

WAR DIARY
or
INTELLIGENCE SUMMARY.
(Erase heading not required.)

No. 2

Place	Date	Hour	Summary of Events and Information	Remarks and references to Appendices
BAIZIEUX	5.VIII.16	10 pm	Clearing up were received by Bn' HQn, which had been W/E, every Sub-section by 2nd Bde from with ADMS. WITTENENCOURT - visited Bn'-Battn. in internment OC. 10th F.A. at their place - en WITTENENCOURT revisited Battn - set a number of latrine at each place & put Infrastructure (order true up cleur lath - Battn Status) - was appointed O.C. Battn.	W.
BAIZIEUX	6.VIII.16	10 pm	visited Battn. at WITTENENCOURT with others - ward to the Brigade troubled with disinfection of emburettes(-) on LAVIEVILLE visited 104th F.A. on FRANVILLERS visited 102nd F.A. - interviewed Dr. Col. IRVINE (O.G.) on anaemic, BAIZIEUX and Col. SKINNER (DDMS) of BRESLE HENENCOURT, MILLENCOURT - Matters of action was Infantine Companions - Two Brigades (111th-112th) such as reinforcements provided - Division Inst. plan 102nd 103rd P.Fld	O.T.
BAIZIEUX	7.VIII.16	10 pm	Rode HENENCOURT, MILLENCOURT tours(y), Matters as of 10&Wmouth Rdn - Inter Division nothing - WITTENENCOURT - Rode on &ALBERT tour(y) for party at 7pm. Saw for front latrine. Matters Sanitary necessity of new Maps at ALBERT O.T.	O.T.
ALBERT	9.VIII.16	10 pm	Rode ALBERT troops Bn' HQ" - made certain sanitary arrangement at ALBERT - Sister tests with other Officers WITTENCOURT at BAIZIEUX when Officers WITTENCOURT in session.	W.

WAR DIARY or INTELLIGENCE SUMMARY

Army Form C. 2118.
No. 3

Place	Date	Hour	Summary of Events and Information	Remarks and references to Appendices
ALBERT	9.VII.16	10 p.m.	Rode MILLENCOURT. Inspected & gave instructions to T.Vs ALBERT. Rode HENENCOURT. Visited Batts. made certain arrangements for disinfestation. Made & instructed Battn. of Lincolnshire. On to BETTENCOURT. D.A.D.O.S. to issue numerocloths (?) to BAIZIEUX Germany (?) for treatment of clothes. To BOVES for walk. To take disinfector round Third Battn. at ALBERT. Section set up Batts. at ALBERT. Made arrangements Sanitary arrangements.	O.K.
ALBERT	10.VII.16	9 p.m.	Interviewed O.C. 104th F.A. regard'g inspection of refuse in vicinity of 104th thickhams. Arranged to have it carted to Divisional Incinerator. Considered certain sanitary arrangements at Aid. Mo.m. for 200 Cavalry from various units who were quartered in bivouacs in grounds of Chateau occupied by Div. M.G.2. Considered various improvements at Aid Batts. in RUE DUBAS at ALBERT. Went with Corporal of 74th Sanitary Section to render transit at water supply in GOWRIE STREET. Rode to FRAMVILLERS & interviewed O.I.C. 102nd F.A. regard'g supply of 3 T.V.s for Div Baths at HENENCOURT & T.V.s for Div Baths at ALBERT to replace one previously supplied by 102nd F.A. — Returned then via to their unit. At 10.30 p.m. to BECOURT CHATEAU regard'g provision of tents, tools, Mats for walk, & gave return from burial parties.	O.K.
ALBERT	11.VII.16		Visited BECOURT CHATEAU at 8 a.m. regard'g provision of disinfection of walks (?) Burial parties — inspected surroundings of 104th FD Ambulance interviewed O.C. & arranged for removal	

Army Form C. 2118.

WAR DIARY
or
INTELLIGENCE SUMMARY.
(Erase heading not required.)

No. 4

Place	Date	Hour	Summary of Events and Information	Remarks and references to Appendices
			Transit of return - Visited Batt. & rode to LAVIEVILLE & interviewed Town Major regards insanitary pool in centre of Village requiring drains; with bailiffs - also interviewed Col. EVANS. S.S.O. 34th Division regards this matter. Rode BECOURT CHATEAU & took 2 N.C.Os of 74th Sanitary Section - 2 T/Us needed attention & unfit for burial parties - 1 car/2 T/Us in charge. Days amount of vermin our clothes disinfected in Foden Disinfector 260 men B3 Division (Notes at Div. Battn. ALBERT.	O.K.
ALBERT	12.VII.16 10 p.m		Visited Div. Baths rode outside arrangement - had A.R.M. 32nd Division round with him to BELLEVUE FARM investigates various insanitary conditions, rearranged for their removal & the provision of Sanitary arrangements. Visited Div. bomb crater rates at Rest of Chateau occupied by 82nd Div. H.Q 2 roomy, well ventilated & kept. After Matinee of Sanitary arrangements. Rode to MILLENCOURT & BAIZIEUX made arrangements Latrines, wash, repair of waterclosets from Baths at ALBERT. Rode in van by 2 No 3 Camp. HENENCOURT WOOD reported a case of Scarlet Fever that had occurred among 1st Lincolns - interviewed R.O. rearranged for Disinfection of hut. Baths 1000 Officer men at Div. Battn	O.K.
ALBERT	13.VII.16 10 p.m		Recalled 5 N.C.Os of Section from MILLENCOURT & ALBERT. Visit Div. Baths made certain arrangements. Walk with 2 C.O BECOURT WOOD - BECOURT CHATEAU, under trees, at upper end of BERKSHIRE AVENUE, advanced pris. station at upper end of NORTHUMBERLAND avenue, rates took in	

WAR DIARY / INTELLIGENCE SUMMARY

Army Form C. 2118. No. 5

Place	Date	Hour	Summary of Events and Information	Remarks and references to Appendices
ALBERT	14.VII.16	10 pm	GOWRE STREET reopened Mun. Station in PERTH AVENUE 10th, water supply, prisoners sanitary conditions - reported to A.D.M.S. myself, water tank in GOWRIE STREET to Major LOCK. Visited latrines in RUE DEBRAY & RUE DE CORBIE that had been repaired etc. in sanitary condition. Paraded for their Bn (who is in a satisfactory state - borrowed T.O's attached to 7th Sanitary Section for Sanitary fatigue work. Batty 1170 Officers there. Ministered clothes (- borrowed items) of clothes for BES Bric. built.	AR
ALBERT	15.VII.16	10 pm	Supervised cleaning of latrines in ALBERT - also gave all Sgts Mn. Batt. - Visited tank in GOWRIE ST. inspected Capt BRODIE OC 221st Coy R.E. (Army Troops) I found that the Major is in the of constructed air-visited latrines in RUE BAPAUME inspected unsatisfactory latrines, parade for supply station of Mypect. latrines (Prisoner) - Visited railway area in ALBERT Pictorial Town Major reports removal of refuse. Inspected railway sanitary units in ALBERT. Most latrine arrangements - With Capt. WAINWRIGHT who visited from advanced Sanitary Officer in ALBERT. Moved him the system that had been adopted by myself. Introduced him to railway part of the main town. Seen his Batts. Purely Station Mr.	AR
ALBERT	16.VII.16	10 pm	Visited BECOURT wood & BECOURT Chateau in district where we are on LA BOISELLE road. Met General carrier Dupont & pursued conditions. Positioned Batts 10 p.m. Battn are coming in trucks (Motor Lorry BRT) - Scale & T.O. are they Gunners coming in German constructed dressing station.	AR

Army Form C. 2118

N° 6

WAR DIARY
or
INTELLIGENCE SUMMARY
(Erase heading not required.)

Instructions regarding War Diaries and Intelligence Summaries are contained in F. S. Regs., Part II and the Staff Manual respectively. Title Pages will be prepared in manuscript.

Place	Date	Hour	Summary of Events and Information	Remarks and references to Appendices
ALBERT	17.viii.16	10 p.m	Visited bivouac at Battn ALBERT & made arrangement for bath, troops coming from trenches - Rode to BEHENCOURT returning DADOS rgarding supply of materials in search for Baths - on to FRANVILLERS & saw O.C. 102nd F.A.	P.R.
ALBERT	18.viii.16	10 p.m	Rode BEHENCOURT. Saw DADOS regarding supply of new underclothes & our undertaking for Baths - to BRESLE in Motor return with Town Major - took ALBERT - Visited BECOURT CHATEAU re allocation in charge of Hospital Sections - Plans for burial parties - Rode to FRANVILLERS & BAIZIEUX. Then made arrangements for Baths at FRANVILLERS and civilian Sanitary arrangements for children. Then on to ALBERT.	
ALBERT	19.viii.16	10.30 a.m	Sent 2 A.C.Os to FRANVILLERS found Shower Baths - Rode HENENCOURT with A.O. & listed reports a number of cases of "fever" also suspicious entire cases - Sent a report to ADMS - Rode in afternoon to BRESLE running up fires up Shower Baths on the following day - On FRANVILLERS rec'd latest work on Baths - to BEHENCOURT near 2 C.O. to hand of ordered repair supply of underclothes for Baths to BAIZIEUX, returning on to MILLENCOURT Battn - to MILLENCOURT returning O.C. D.S.C. Infants Ques: Water tested - Hot FRANVILLERS Battn - to MILLENCOURT & interviewed Town Major regarding supply of towels. Referred to ADMS (Indian) orders for removal from BAIZIEUX in case - interviewed Colonel CHANCE at 30th Div. H.Q. regarding orders to supply Bers. & FRANVILLERS on return - July 11th 1916 Reply July 19 1916 to advise 6333 and we heard at first. Should they from July 11th 1916 L/Cpl Pte Battn droug at their usages - Bers - be at ALBERT all the 32nd burials of the men attacked 24th but were returning a day, be shut & sent to have known troops T. Noster & sent the war scattered has been replaced to BOVES left ward twenty seriously and sleep sick	(R.

1875 Wt. W 593/826 1,000,000 4/15 J.B.C. & A. A.D.S.S./Forms/C. 2118.

WAR DIARY or INTELLIGENCE SUMMARY

Army Form C. 2118

No. 7

Place	Date	Hour	Summary of Events and Information	Remarks and references to Appendices
BAIZIEUX	20.VIII.16	10 pm	Sanitary Section HQn to BAIZIEUX - Set up Shower-baths at BRESLE & FRANVILLERS & command Water troops - Shown Divn Hdqrs by Lt Col FRANVILLERS Remained there after Settling in. Visited MILLENCOURT & saw O.C. 10th Fd Amb(W) at Battn area & this week on public duty.	CAR.
BAIZIEUX	21.VIII.16	10 pm	Went with A.D.M.S. to FRANVILLERS inspected division of bath - interviewed Col IRVINE O.C. 10th Wst Yk. on to BRESLE re visited bath. Fa HENENCOURT with A.D.M.S. interviewed O.C. 103rd Fd (WILLEGETWOOD). Inspected Camp in HENENCOURT WOOD. Visited FRANVILLERS & BRESLE re visits & works of bath & arrang for bath of troops.	
BAIZIEUX	22.VIII.16	10 am	Visited FRANVILLERS re visited bath & visited DRS made arrangement for erection of shower bath - on to HENENCOURT & saw Staff Captain of 101st Inf Bde re what & sites for erection of shower bath re - on to MILLENCOURT & saw O.C. 10th Fd. Hist'd baths - on to BEHENCOURT Tarain(W) with 112th Bde re erect shower bath - had crater arrangements re laying supply water for shower baths.	CAR.
BAIZIEUX	23.VIII.16	11 am	Re FRANVILLERS re visited baths on to BEHENCOURT Tarain(W) for erection of shower bath after interviewing Camp Commandant (Col ROSE) of 111th Coy at MONTIGNY - thereby thence to General Sir INGOUVILLE WILLIAMS at WARLOY - Rtr to MILLENCOURT & thence baths & to BRESLE re same baths.	CAR.
BAIZIEUX	24.VIII.16	10 am	Visited BEHENCOURT Tarain(W) to attend 2RCos, for Sanitary duty, w/ 8th Bn North'bn Battn - on FRANVILLERS & visited baths & 102nd F.A. - made reverse arrangements regards baths & laundries.	CAR.
BAIZIEUX	25.VIII.16	11 am	Visited baths at BRESLE & FRANVILLERS & made reverse arrangements also interviewed R.O. & L.O. of 111th/14th Bde re Sanitary matters - Visited 101st Bde HQd at HENENCOURT & saw Bde Major & Staff Captain re arranged for baths, 10th chair & 16th Royal Scot in billets daily distrib hot baths reduced to. Visited baths at MILLENCOURT arranged for fitting up of Royal Rs on Xdm day - Visited bath arrangement for this at MILLENCOURT baths shown (W) - Battn Visited 15th Royal Scot & 11th Suffolks on 27.VIII.16. 10.45 pm - spoke to Staff Captain 101st Bde re telephone re shortage of 8000 men on platoon duty.	CAR.

1875 Wt. W593/826 1,000,000 4/15 J.B.C. & A. A.D.S.S./Forms/C. 2118.

Army Form C. 2118

WAR DIARY or INTELLIGENCE SUMMARY

No. 8

Place	Date	Hour	Summary of Events and Information	Remarks and references to Appendices
Harte BAIZIEUX	26.iii.16	11/h	Bn(?) 2000 arr of 10th Lincolns 716th Royal Scots issued accoutrements & rifles to late arrivals. 10th returned in late after breakfast, visited Baths at MILLENCOURT, BRESLE, FRANVILLERS. Submitted Bath arrangements to Divisl. Camp. in HENENCOURT. Work on existing 10th Lincolns 716th Royal Scots ranged(?) the huts. That Battn. cleaned out 15 May (?). Visited BEHENCOURT Baths, interviewed Town Major.	OK
BAIZIEUX	27.iii.16	11/h	Battn 2150 arr. of 15th Royal Scots & 11th Suffolks. Architect letter R. — Visited BRESLE Trains, Baths ready(?) for Bath. Prayers(?) of (?). Clothes — also to Bn of a Queens Regt (Pte(?) Parath(?)) (?) made at the Baths at BRESLE.	OK
BAIZIEUX	28.iii.16	8/h	Visited BEHENCOURT saw Town Major. Visited billet occupied by 6th Bedfords & 9th Earl Rams. Repeated position of his Jill(?) Ladies. Visited BRESLE Baths produced billet required are required by 13 Royal Fusiliers & 18th K.R.R. Interview on Os. on & Baths of FRANVILLERS. That little arrangement.	OK
BAIZIEUX	29.iii.16	9/h	Visited 101st Bde E. HENENCOURT with sen. D.O. 15th Royal Scots officers — Saunders, Austin – Reber, visited FRANVILLERS, BRESLE, BEHENCOURT required Baths. 7 Buses on after.	OK
BAIZIEUX	30.iii.16	10/h	Visited ALBERT That arrangement for over Baths (chimney) Hate over the situation in RUE DUBAS on fg of Division — Visited situation of Camp. Stretcher by BLE Buis May on the West Side of the btn ALBERT — DERNANCOURT (E.G.(?)(?)) Rules(?) Saw(?) Rly arrangement. Visited Baths at BRESLE, FRANVILLERS — (?) 7 Vaudan(?), So ft. Red Rats Stuck recover on following day — Hadon charge	OK
ALBERT	31.iii.16	10/h	Batt forced up at ALBERT. Rented Hqrs to 12 RUE DE BRAY in ALBERT T.sd.(?) Baths in RUE DUBAS — Visited camp & met &c. Division of HQrs 34 into & ADMS — members of relative(?) enjoyed in Amvantic(?), presents(?) Baths of Sanitary upn in camp of Gulliver at HQ D.	OK

W.B.S.(?) Cafe(?) R.N. C.T.

34th Div.

SECRET
Original/Duplicate

WAR DIARY

of

o/c. 74th SANITARY SECTION

for

AUGUST 1916.

VOLUME N° 8.   PAGES 5.

COMMITTEE FOR THE
MEDICAL HISTORY OF THE WAR
Date -9 OCT 1916

WAR DIARY or INTELLIGENCE SUMMARY

Army Form C. 2118

Place	Date	Hour	Summary of Events and Information	Remarks and references to Appendices
ALBERT	1.viii.16	8 pm	Visited Divisional HQrs & individual Sanitary unit. His duties carried out by Section, reports to ADMS. Asst Sanitary Officer of ALBERT & nature Town Major & turned in various matters - (Plans) birth other incidents for Sanitary viii permit at HQ2 - Visited Divl HQ 2 a.m - evg	CWS
ALBERT	2.viii.16	10 p.m	Rode to Camp of 34th Divisional HQ2. Rsup visited Sanitary work being carried out by the Sanitary Section - Photo ADMS. Visited ADMS area around Mnetz MAMETZ wood (in its a number of shellers) various [illegible] Thu huts in unfit water hand - also in relation a well stored for them reports at the S.W end MAMETZ wood & found it of little in unsuit for use as Sanitary Shelters - Reports their quarters ADMS	CWS
ALBERT	3.viii.16	10 p.m	Rode recon. Horse Rifle with that evening a showed get in camp - Visited site ADMS to BECOURT wood – various articles which led him reports to leave up - took back to HQ & the [illegible] up then & BAIZIEUX later to LONELY COPSE to all of R.C. of FRICOURT visited 34 Divl Damp. Various & for situation of Quick lime burial to [illegible] sanitary shelter Visited Class 3 HQrs & they burial at 7.30 & various areas for ADMS repart – various points for BECOURT wood. Read a Mem. Pay.	CWS
ALBERT	4.viii.16	10 p.m	Went to BECOURT WOOD Rsup visited work of 1st ann Rep. fichment [and] FRECHENCOURT cleaning up the area. Reported ADMS. Rode to Divl. Damp - Lonely Copse near FRICOURT Riport [illegible]	CWS
ALBERT	5.viii.16	6 p.m	Supervised work of Saniturists (two men) in BECOURT WOOD - also visited Plates, rush ali- Reported CWS
ALBERT	6.viii.16	10 p.m	Reported to ADMS at 8 am At ALBERT had twi heavy Addm tuni with irregul [illegible] Itens preview at Bath House Rite Prokr Many trains to place - advance up for chain in headquarter of 111 Bn Sau Sec to be [illegible] in RUE DU MOULIN A L'HUILE [illegible] selected, Buts. Motor Mc fuller on the truck of the time from RUE DE FONTAINE - Visited BECOURT Went to advice work was for Police intactor.	CWS

1875 Wt. W593/826 1,000,000 4/15 J.B.C. & A. A.D.S.S./Forms/C. 2118.

WAR DIARY
or
INTELLIGENCE SUMMARY

Army Form C. 2118

2

Place	Date	Hour	Summary of Events and Information	Remarks and references to Appendices
ALBERT	7.VIII.16	10 p.m	Move Show fruth from RUE DUBAS, also from Rue fructur Remy, place of being uum shortly R.W. of bridge to RUE DE LA FONTAINE, on W. side of river & on outskirts of ALBERT – Supervised erection of hats & 7 Canvas Screens (re Royal S.) A.D.M.S. visited BECOURT WOODS & advised rgt of cleaning up. We have arrangement with O.C. 10th Royal Scots of that battalion on Phone – Ry the O.C. 11th Suffolks & Hoath battalion on 9.VIII.16. This battalion were occupying BECOURT WOOD cellars &c in trenches.	OK
ALBERT	8.VIII.16	9.30 p.m	Supervised work of Truth - Noted & A.D.M.S. In afternoon went to BECOURT WOODS to visit what B. A.D.M.S. on west front & found C. to work requiring attention - also a report at the Gth Mortuary being this area in a Scott factory cmdshn.	OK
ALBERT	9.VIII.16	9 p.m	Inspected Camp of 176 Br R.F.A. on ALBERT- AMIENS road and from ALBERT with R.O. - inspected work at the Baths - Indented with the BECOURT WOODS. Reported to A.D.M.S.	OK
ALBERT	10.VIII.16	7.30 p.m	Reported to A.D.M.S. at 9.15 – visited Division of Baths & interviewed Town Major ALBERT re suitable supply of light men for general sanitary purposes in ALBERT at 6. p.m. today. Risk Royal Scots made arrangement for taking full battalion on the 11th - also secured various Sanitary men from – inspected took over from in BECOURT WOODS rund arrangement for battle g in rear vacatins	OK
ALBERT	11.VIII.16	9.30 p.m	Rec Report BAZENTIN LE PETIT Woods and near Maure (not seen) Also near Maure (not seen) MAMETZ Wood in QUADRANGLE (wood) to be surrounded (proved) around FRICOURT & LOZENGE WOOD (all at BECOURT WOOD – infantry work here - Baths &c new to public latrine drinkers - Supply &c - supply throughout with 10th 15th &c Royal Scots	OK
ALBERT	12.VIII.16	9.30 p.m	Reported to A.D.M.S. - Discussing Repairs &c - supply throughout with divisional area - visited Burial &c huts in the afternoon inspected work done in latrines hats in BECOURT WOODS - general condition of that area	OK

Army Form C. 2118

WAR DIARY
or
INTELLIGENCE SUMMARY
(Erase heading not required.)

Instructions regarding War Diaries and Intelligence Summaries are contained in F. S. Regs., Part II. and the Staff Manual respectively. Title Pages will be prepared in manuscript.

Remarks and references to Appendices: **3**

Place	Date	Hour	Summary of Events and Information	Remarks
ALBERT	13.viii.16	10 p.m	Prict Sanitary Officer of 12th Division at B.H.Q. Divisional HQ returned to ALBERT with him later, with complete report. Afterwards showed him Poicardi. BECOURT WOODS shown him area with complete report. Afterwards visited various matters. ALBERT occupied by 5th Sanitary Section - Divisional Baths - Visiting various matters. Taraki — the burial of bodies. The afternoon took to BECOURT WOODS made arrangements for sitting up screw fallen with him. BRESLE, FRANVILLERS, LA HOUSSOYE — Took over (late of Div.) HQ) 23rd Div section at water butts, from section to BRESLE.	C.R.T.
BAIZIEUX	14.viii.16	10.30 p.m	Took over quarters at ALBERT — Removed from Division to Baizieux — FRANVILLERS removed to Baizieux Market for 102nd F.A. Removed HQ. of 7th Sanitary Section to BAIZIEUX. Slept above matter at BRESLE, FRANVILLERS, LA HOUSSOYE — Handed over all disinfected clothes to O.C. Laundry — Saw clean cloth from DADOS disinfected & returned to ADMS.	C.R.T.
BAIZIEUX	15.viii.16	10 p.m	Visited bath at BRESLE FRANVILLERS LA HOUSSOYE. Whist at Brigade HQ re arrangements for Battn of Infantry Brigade, returning a member of men of Infantry Brigade at BRESLE & FRANVILLERS — For Disinfector in un-disinfected cloth.	C.R.T.
BAIZIEUX	16.viii.16	10 p.m	Visited baths at BRESLE FRANVILLERS LA HOUSSOYE Supervised work & supply of cloth. Disinfection of cloth, also accounts for attendance of baths further.	C.R.T.
BAIZIEUX	17.viii.16	10 p.m	Visited baths at BRESLE FRANVILLERS LA HOUSSOYE. Arranged for their trip from town ready for removal to LA HOUSSOYE — The French hospital for Infantry who had failed to receive any disinfected cloth. Saw Colonel CHANCE re arrangement for disposal of disinfected cloth.	C.R.T.
HALLENCOURT	18.viii.16	10 p.m	Proceeded to HALLENCOURT to ERGUINGHEM. Visited baths at FRANVILLERS, BRESLE, LA HOUSSOYE. Took arrangements for their removal — HQ of 7th Sanitary Section moved to HALLENCOURT.	
HALLENCOURT	19.viii.16	10 p.m	Removed from here HQ of HALLENCOURT.	C.R.T.
HALLENCOURT	20.viii.16	11 a.m	Sanitary Section moved to PONT REMY for entrainment.	C.R.T.

WAR DIARY or INTELLIGENCE SUMMARY

Army Form C. 2118

(Erase heading not required.)

Place	Date	Hour	Summary of Events and Information	Remarks and references to Appendices
DOULIEU	21.viii.16	7 pm	Arrived BAILLEUL at 2 a.m. Met Sanitary Section. Returned to DOULIEU arriving 4 a.m. – Section enjoyed erected latrines re furniture at Mq DivSion at TURBI-Vichy CROIX DU BAC Saw ADMS Mq 16th Division. Interviewed Mq 34th Division.	Obs.
DOULIEU	22.viii.16	9 pm	Rode CROIX DU BAC interviewed Sanitary Officer of 18th Division Mq about Sanitary work in area – Plans & inspection of 18th Sanitary Section engaged in Sanitary work at CROIX DU BAC + ERQUINGHEM. Visited various places in new area. Roman RC Section	Obs.
DOULIEU	23.viii.16	9 pm	Rode CROIX DU BAC + ERQUINGHEM interviewed Sanitary Officer of 18th Division. Inspection of work. Made arrangements for works in general.	Obs. Obs.
CROIX DU BAC	24.viii.16	7.30 pm	Army HQ + CROIX DU BAC + Minto & ADMS - Visited BAC ST MAUR & ERQUINGHEM. Made interior arrangements for billets and area.	Obs.
CROIX DU BAC	25.viii.16	9.30 am	Visited BAC ST MAUR + CROIX DU BAC. Inspected work done at latter place. Took arrangements with new Sanitary Section in that area.	Obs.
CROIX DU BAC	26.viii.16	9.30 pm	Reports to ADMS afterwards for Sanitary work in CROIX DU BAC. Paid civilian workmen in CROIX DU BAC rafterwards ERQUINGHEM visited part of that latter place with Senior R.O.	Obs.
CROIX DU BAC	27.viii.16	7 pm	Visited various units in CROIX DU BAC. Inspected work carried out by Sanitary Section – In afternoon went to Divisional Baths. Afterwards Laundries and places for Divisional Baths.	Obs.
CROIX DU BAC	28.viii.16	7 pm	Visited CROIX DU BAC. Inspected work done in morning. In afternoon – Corporal + 4 T.U.s engaged in clearing out etc. Forward Villages – Visited Transport Lines of 152nd + 176th Brigade R.F.A. also of 102nd Machine Gun Coy.	Obs.
CROIX DU BAC	29.viii.16	7.30 pm	Visited CROIX DU BAC. Inspected ADMS – in afternoon visited ERQUINGHEM + ROLANDERIE FARM. Made arrangements with Staff Captain 101st Inf. Bde. for cleaning huts and cleaning up latrines in area.	Obs.
CROIX DU BAC	30.viii.16	7.30 pm	Visited ROLANDERIE FARM. Inspected work done by latrine party of 40 men under O.C. of Sanitary Section.	Obs.

1875 Wt. W593/826 1,000,000 4/15 J.B.C. & A. A.D.S.S./Forms/C. 2118.

WAR DIARY
or
INTELLIGENCE SUMMARY

Army Form C. 2118

(Erase heading not required.)

Place	Date	Hour	Summary of Events and Information	Remarks and references to Appendices
CROIX DU BAC	31.VIII.16	7.30pm	Visited ERQUINGHEM & ARMENTIERES - visited Cesspool at ERQUINGHEM & several billets. Made arrangements for their further supervision - In afternoon visited CROIX DU BAC & Divisional Instruction Camp near SAILLY concerning various Sanitary matters.	

(signed) Edward Capt. R.A.M.C.T.
O.C. 74th Sanitary Section

140/817

SECRET
Sept. 1916

WAR — DIARY
of
O/c 11th SANITARY SECTION
3rd DIVISION

SEPTEMBER 1916

Vol. No. 9.   pages 4

COMMITTEE FOR THE
MEDICAL HISTORY OF THE WAR
Date -9 DEC. 1915

WAR DIARY
or
INTELLIGENCE SUMMARY
(Erase heading not required.)

Army Form C. 2118

Place	Date	Hour	Summary of Events and Information	Remarks and references to Appendices
CROIX DU BAC	1.IX.16	7.30 p.m	Visited various Billets at Troops in CROIX DU BAC (raggis, the neighbourhood) - In afternoon visited various Camps of 34th Division at Hammond of Qum. near R.O.	ADS.
CROIX DU BAC	2.IX.16	7.30 p.m	Visited various units in CROIX DU BAC ragging for sanitary in morning left the roads. In afternoon visited ROLANDERIE FARM - ?Gilbert? Garage in mornings also ERQUINGHEM & visited 102nd Machine Gun Section - Paid final view at CROIX DU BAC ERQUINGHEM - Visited 104th ?North? Ambulance at L'ESTRADE - Saw how fires for sterilizer in camp of 104th F.A.	ADS.
CROIX DU BAC	3.IX.16	7.30 p.m	Visited RUE MARLE rest point area with R.O. 21st Northumberland Fusiliers Turned out for sanitary work & to stay by fatigue parties of So T.Us on following days. In afternoon went to 102nd Field Ambulance Parmentier with Colonel IRVINE for 50 T.Us at out at RUE MARLE in following morn.	ADS.
CROIX DU BAC	4.IX.16	7.30 p.m	Visited RUE MARLE transferred work point. Sent by fatigue party also a number of Huts & Nunnery - Visited Rolanderie Farm occupied by 101st F.A. Br. Inspected work done by Sanitary Section on huts also Borings visited camp occupied by 102nd Machine Gun Coy.	ADS.
CROIX DU BAC	5.IX.16	7.30 p.m	Visited RUE MARLE rest pt - In p.m. visited occupations of the cuisine loft room at farm Camp occupied by Tomas; also visited R.O. for accommodation	ADS.
CROIX DU BAC	6.IX.16	7.30 p.m	?Arrow officer with Baron Thorgnies? held now heads of T.Us - Received helio Coy of 104th F.A. & ?Sharp pictures? within afternoon 6th Baron Thorgnies. Sent by T.Us visited Camp of 102nd Machine Gun Coy.	ADS.
CROIX DU BAC	7.IX.16	8.30 p.m	Rode RUE MARLE rest pt. visited work T.Us South Side of ERQUINGHEM - BAC ST MAUR Road - Rode BAILLEUL ?avered? culverts (sanitary Sector - on to HQ of VIIIth Corps made Colonel GERRARD DDMS 8th Corps meeting with him at YPRES.	ADS.
CROIX DU BAC	8.IX.16	8 p.m	Visited various Billets pts in CROIX DU BAC - in afternoon rode to ROLANDERIE FARM inspected work recently completed on Canteen Farm & LA VESEE in which Billets occupied by 10th R.Celtics on were - on to ?Trenches? Talo occupied by 16th Royal Scots Marche R.O. (D.S. ?Col?. GILMORE) in which also water supplies in trenches.	ADS.
CROIX DU BAC	9.IX.16	5 p.m	?About? BILLET Farm — on ERQUINGHEM returned R.O. in charge at HQ of Subsection (sanitary) RUE MARLE rest point work done. Made ?new? account for Employs of empties & lamps on + ERQUINGHEM Read Cardiac & Subsection of Sanitary Sector. Made Collies carrying unit - Paid visit to DADMS DU BAC visited ?cutter? West at CROIX DU BAC. Rode to PROVEN to HQ of VIIIth Corps. to see Col: GERRARD — DADMS	ADS.

WAR DIARY
or
INTELLIGENCE SUMMARY

Army Form C. 2118

Place	Date	Hour	Summary of Events and Information	Remarks and references to Appendices
CROIX DU BAC	11.IX.16	6 pm	Returned from PROVEN — reported to ADMS. Visited various billets — CROIX DU BAC. Tried arrangements for sanitary work.	OUT
CROIX DU BAC	12.IX.16	9 pm	Went with Water Duty Corporal (Horace Thurles). Photo inspected all water supplies for some interval, Rte. Dr. + various [illegible] Bu(llets[?]) interior.	OUT
CROIX DU BAC	13.IX.16	6 pm	Went with ADMS round — FORT ROMPU, BAC ST MAUR, RUE MARLE, ROLANDERIE, various their areas — Rte to BOIS GRENIER re-visited water supply at BREWERY pumping station, Rte to WHITE CITY + photo water at standpipe — with view to refills of water troughs.	OUT
(CROIX DU BAC 14.IX.16)				
CROIX DU BAC	14.IX.16	6 pm	Reported ADMS — visited insanitary billets occupied by 34th Bn. Signaller reported to ADMS. Rte RUE MARLE, ERQUINGHEM, FORT ROMPU + BAC ST MAUR — visited a number of camps, billets interviewed R.M.O.s 2nd + 1st Lancs R.G.A.	OUT
CROIX DU BAC	15.IX.16	6 pm	Visited the Trai. Bt. 12 Pioneer with R.M.O. & chief sit for centre of Shower Bath — (arr. for Batt. render[?] Rawi. — inspected (Road DU BAC site.	OUT
CROIX DU BAC	16.IX.16	6 pm	Dm. BAILLEUL for cash to pay various labourers — on to ERQUINGHEM. Flew arrived to RUE GRENIER. Photo water supply — on FORT ROMPU Road have care of Latrines completed in a division stand Farm — Bund Farm — thru [?] to ..... reported to DADMS @ 1 PM + Town Major of ERQUINGHEM. (20 C 33 (31:36) Helio at on to French — reported to DMS.	OUT
CROIX DU BAC	17.IX.16	6 pm	Visited Camps reinforced by 152nd RFA. BB1 major [?] 160 RFA. (15th)-B1 Wagon Lines — 30th Batt (TQ[?]) — 1.2 & B section.	OUT
CROIX DU BAC	18.IX.16	6 pm	Visited Wagon Lines, 154th RFA. B.C. [?] 160 RFA (1 to 11) + B B.U. — 175th RFA + B1 Wagon —	OUT
CROIX DU BAC	19.IX.16	6 pm	Visited today, re-visited the water supplies in trenches occupied by 34th Division [illegible] rebuilt + [?].	OUT
CROIX DU BAC	20.IX.16	6 pm	Reported to Mil. [illegible] Scheme for water supply of Trenches — visited RUE MARLE — tried various billets recently vacated by 34th + ... — to ARMENTIERES with view to — on to ARMEE. Made [illegible] met after arrangements for centering the part at RUE MARLE.	OUT

1875 Wt. W593/826 1,000,000 4/15 J.B.C. & A. A.D.S.S./Forms/C. 2118.

Army Form C. 2118

WAR DIARY
or
INTELLIGENCE SUMMARY
(Erase heading not required.)

3

Place	Date	Hour	Summary of Events and Information	Remarks and references to Appendices
CROIX DU BAC	21.IX.16	8 p.m.	Visited Trenches in R(L) Sector occupied by 20th Northumberland Fusiliers resp. visited Dugout recently occupied by contents of a case of Diphtheria — instructed M.O. to have it thoroughly disinfected — also visited two other Dugouts that had been occupied by 2 cases of Diphtheria — visited their Billets & enquired when cases of RUE MARLE – L'ARMÉE & CHAPELLE D'ARMENTIÈRES reported ADMS. attended Conference of Sanitary Officers of ARMENTIÈRES with reference to totals over that area.	AR
CROIX DU BAC	22.IX.16	6 p.m.	Visited various Camps on FORT ROMPU – ERQUINGHEM road. Inspected systems re. of latrines &c. in same, trough of closing of Camps – Visited various Bivouac hut Camps that occupied by trench Party of 8th Durham L.I. in BAC. saw these very nicely kept — that on opposite side, Inspected wash house in Camp near FORT ROMPU Oce. attended Water Board Meeting 2.30 p.m. at Offices of BAILLEUL – visited ERQUINGHEM TRUE MARLE 11 A.M. Civilians, Temporary health & Sanitn — inspected two Baths occupied by trenches of Dhipleria.	AR
CROIX DU BAC	23.IX.16	6 p.m.	Visited ROLANDERIE FARM CANTEEN FARM, BOIS GRENIER Brwy, in these Kit 1 Bttn. 8 army Water Supplies – inspected steam pipes in ARMENTIÈRES (water camp) reused by 2-1 Londs R.G.A. at FORT ROMPU. inspected water supplies at ESTAIRES – DOULIEU M inspd. ADMS – Visited ARMENTIÈRES & returning Town Major Sanitary Officer – in visited Factory in RUE DE PAIX recently vacated by 25th	AR
CROIX DU BAC	26.IX.16	6 p.m.	Gottenham'sanitation reported same to Mayor Sanitary Officer. Visited RUE MARLE inspected various Billet & 102nd Bijour (in ARMENTIÈRES Report accoutrements). In Baths. Circuit at RUE MARLE visited Billet of Y. 2nd Gordons in an unsatisfactory condition. Used 6 Bath. ST MAURT ERQUINGHEM & his billet cleared the field that 2 few trenches by man in 2nd 11th Lances infantry bn. discovery. TRUE MARLE 6 102w Br 11 Bn. Inspd. Enquired Haut(?) own in 21st ASH where from.	AR
CROIX DU BAC	27.IX.16	6 p.m.	Went to RUE MARLE Visited HQ f. 102w Br. Marles various cases of Sickness – visited NIC & his Betta hut. recently ordered by B–m who an interim from acute Diphtheria – visited Pt. south in	AR

1875 |Wt. W593/826 1,000,000 4/15 J.B.C. & A. A.D./S.S./Forms/C. 2118.

WAR DIARY
or
INTELLIGENCE SUMMARY

Army Form C. 2118

Place	Date	Hour	Summary of Events and Information	Remarks and references to Appendices
CROIX DU BAC	26.IX.16	6 p.m.	Trenches occupied by men of 21st & 22nd Q.F.s 770 the Lieut. who were returned from Birkenhead & acute Nephritis - has this all returned by direct rail return to the O. duties. Visited hospital station at BOIS GRENIER rd.post & with 16th Royal Scots near ROLANDERIE Farm - visited various units at RUE MARLE & ERQUINGHEM. Visited RAMC & camp occupied by A Tr.Bu 160 RFA - HQ & with Q.O.	OK
CROIX DU BAC	29.IX.16	8 p.m.	Visited HQ 34th Divl. Train transferred to billets recently occupied by men returning from acute Nephritis.	OK
CROIX DU BAC	30.IX.16	7 p.m.	Saw Sanitary Sect (Capt Figgins) & area occupied by 103rd Brigade also area around ARMENTIERES. Visited billets of various units returning from Brigade in rest — some of these are not very satisfactory & are liable to cause infection if men in them contact disease. PONT NIEPPE — visited billets and baths. Then to Force at Mine — water of Brewery — Bac St Maur was — Pont de Nieppe — Bac St Maur — Erquinghem — Bac St Maur — Report to A.D.M.S.	OK

W. Crozier Capt. R.Mc.C.T.
O.C. 7th Sanitary Section

140/1811

WAR — DIARY.
of
O/c. 7th. SANITARY - SECTION
34th DIVISION

Vol. No. 10.   PAGES 4

October 1916.

Serial
Oct. 1916

COMMITTEE FOR THE
MEDICAL HISTORY OF THE WAR
Date −9 DEC. 1916

Army Form C. 2118

WAR DIARY
or
INTELLIGENCE SUMMARY
(Erase heading not required.)

Instructions regarding War Diaries and Intelligence Summaries are contained in F.S. Regs., Part II. and the Staff Manual respectively. Title Pages will be prepared in manuscript.

Place	Date	Hour	Summary of Events and Information	Remarks and references to Appendices
CROIX DU BAC	1.X.16	6 pm	Visited H.Q. of B/FC 34th Bde & interviewed A.O. Discussed avoidance of drain hospitals, in build-West on 6 to 4 Section turn of the Field Ambulances. Newly occupied by new sections. Arrangements – also prepare – on to PONT NIEPPE Finished built used by Franks force at present under Major (Colonel Richmond) O.C. 103rd Field Ambulance, interviewing him them. Inspected various camps also ERQUINGHEM – BAC ST MAUR roads. Reported to ADMS.	Off.
CROIX DU BAC	2.X.16	7.30 pm	Attended at Orderly room 53rd Battery RFA. & situated in RUE BLANCHE & gave evidence against a man for drunk. Mess. Ref. on to H.Q. 1/L 152nd Bde RFA – also R.O. Visit of Capt. & GRIS POT & various arrangements for men refreshing from advanced positions – arranged for this future of Field – worn on to 104 F.A. positioned OC.	Off.
CROIX DU BAC	3.X.16	8 pm	Gave lectures to Sanitary men + Water bearers at division of Instructional School. Made an enemy of Officer I/C/s on Sanitation after same place.	Off.
CROIX DU BAC	4.X.16	7 pm	Visited Field Dr at RUE MARLE newly occupied by new refresh from advanced positions. Arrangements for (space?) the Reference of men – inspired into outcomes. Gave lectures in 212 A.T. Railway (?) to Sanitation & Water bearers.	Off.
CROIX DU BAC	5.X.16	6 pm	Visited various areas in STEENWERCKE with Lt. DAVIES M.I 104 F.A. (Sanitation Officer) – Visited DAC HQ inspected Sanitation Cond. – Gave lectures in Sanitation & Water bearers at Div Instruction School. Visited A.T. – interviewed A.D.	Off.
CROIX DU BAC	6.X.16	6 pm	Visited Pumping Station W/ BOIS GRENIER, also WHITE CITY WATER FARM (new water supply) with MADRAS Sap. Off. – Gave lectures in Sanitation & Water bearers in RUE MARLE. Visit of Bde 166 Bde RFA at CHAPELLE ARMENTIERES reported, a case of infect syphilis.	Off.
CROIX DU BAC	7.X.16	8 pm	Visited various Field Ambulances applied for by 16th Royal Scots in RUE DEL PIERRE. with A.O. Visited Au Anti-mosquitos Parades & Schools in Flanders – lectured and R.O. Paul Section & (details?) Reported worked on	Off.

Army Form C. 2118

WAR DIARY
or
INTELLIGENCE SUMMARY
(Erase heading not required.)

Place	Date	Hour	Summary of Events and Information	Remarks and references to Appendices
CROIX DU BAC	5.X.16	6 pm	Visited CROIX DU BAC village — letter to RUE MARLE & wife to be killed recently mauled by car. Referred him to 206 City R.E. — interviewed R.O. 15th R.F. regarding reward for two waterrats, yellow matter.	CWR
CROIX DU BAC	9.XI.16	7 pm	Visited RUE MARLE — saw R.O. of 16th — N.F. re marks (sanitary matter — visited 27 — R.F. re trench marks, 2 cases of dysentery from front billets, spoke out with R.O. arranged for enquiry on typhoid R.E. in trenches. Saw R.A.O.	CWR
CROIX DU BAC	10.X.16	7 h	Went ARMENTIERES (interviewed) Colonel LEGETWOOD — O.C. 103rd F.A. made inspection of Estaminets (regn) than that were emptied. Contributed Mushroom elond on to prevention of a future Kinan. In quite 1 killed at Blue Blend Pantry — ARMENTIERES that had been occupied by Privates 15th-R.F. who had been sent to hospital with suspect typhoid. Inspected a number of Estaminets at ERQUINGHEM & FORT ROMPU. Plan in attention, marks drain of (part re) inspected Estaminet at L'ARMEE BOISGRENIER, RUE DELATREE, ERQUINGHEM & FORT ROMPU r, with institution marks, precaution against a future known, mark, ADMS.	CWR
CROIX DU BAC	12.XI.16	7.30 pm	Visited STEENWERCKE T'ESTRADE — inspected camp occupied by C. By 175th R.F.A. T.T. Visited H.Q. of 160th R.F. R.F.A. at RUE MARLE re mark, application for waterscatter, referred to Visited A.B.C. it Belturme.	CWR
CROIX DU BAC	13.XI.16	7.30 pm	Visited No 2 Sector & 175 BAC re dysentery killed recently emptied by men suffering from disentry (true ditty) Authorities — interviewed CRE 34th Div for marks — did key for on willie can do (tractable) — visited (Ullerie) visited ERQUINGHEM temporary Streets as manufacturing H. Doar Gagin — in particular Surgeon Secretary, marks was / James Carl	CWR

1875 Wt. W 593/826 1,000,000 4/15 J.B.C. & A. A.D.S.S./Forms/C. 2118.

WAR DIARY
or
INTELLIGENCE SUMMARY

Army Form C. 2118

Place	Date	Hour	Summary of Events and Information	Remarks and references to Appendices
CROIX DU BAC	14.X.16	7.30p.m.	Inspected water supplies at BOIS GRENIER pumping station, WHITE CITY, BIRD CAGE TRAMLINE AVENUE & COWGATE AVENUE - Interviewed R.O. of 11th Suffolks repair/nature accommodation in trenches.	A.T.
CROIX DU BAC	15.X.16	7.30p.m.	Inspected water supplies at LILLE POST, CHARDS FARM, BURNT FARM, WINE AVENUE, PARADISE ALLEY & THE SALIENT	A.T.
CROIX DU BAC	16.X.16	7.30p.m.	Inspected new Postern Baths. R of R.E. re PETIT MORTIER - Reported B.A.D.M.S. & Sanitary Tank water supplies. Inspected Billets in RUE DORMOIRE that had been flooded. Out of flooded area - (Cnr Flyplan) Inspected various water supplies at PETRONNEL BOIS GRENIER	A.T.
CROIX DU BAC	17.X.16	7.30p.m.	Visited ERQUINGHEM - Interviewed Rayont Scanlon with Town Mayor Rayont in Main Boulevard and at RUE HAS - on to HQrs of 16th Royal Scots at ROLANDERIE was shortly held by enemy. Then in RUE DELATRE - interviewed R.O. of 11th Royal Scots - Visited 8th DAC HQrs returned R.O. to H.Q. in various camp of No 3 Section HQrs Section.	A.T.
CROIX DU BAC	18.X.16	7.30p.m.	Visited HQrs & Sections of S.D.T.C. with M.Os - also various lines of 152nd, 760 Bde R.F.A. paying official attention that Millets. Visited 10.45 p.m. Reserve ordnance stores reports some of M.D.S. B.C. 8th Division.	A.T.
CROIX DU BAC	19.X.16	7.30p.m.	Visited D-Battery 152 R.F.A. various lines, & HQrs & No. 1 Section of DAC. Gave lecture on Sanitation at Divisional Instructional School.	A.T.
CROIX DU BAC	20.X.16	7.30p.m.	Visited water supplies in Right Sector of trenches with G.O.C. & A.D.M.S. 34th Division - RR. ERQUINGHEM & saw R.C.D. in charge of Sanitation (Sanitary Man lecture on Sanitation)	A.T.
CROIX DU BAC	21.X.16	7.30p.m.	Visited BOIS GRENIER Pumping Station & Billets, MDS & arrangements for billet party at ERQUINGHEM - Inspected Billets occupied by O.C. in RUE DES ACQUETS - Paid Cartilevi & Sanitation (Sanitary Men) & Sections HQrs at ROLANDERIE Particular RAC, & 110th Infantry Brigade HAD. & 10 Bde. Section DAC. at LE GRAND BEAUMART - RAK in RUE DELPIERRE re Billets. Reported on hospital TADMS.	A.T.

1875 Wt. W593/826 1,000,000 4/15 J.B.C. & A. A.D.S.S./Forms/C. 2118.

WAR DIARY
INTELLIGENCE SUMMARY

Army Form C. 2118

Place	Date	Hour	Summary of Events and Information	Remarks and references to Appendices
CROIX DU BAC	22.X.16	7.30 p.m	Visited Transport Lines at 21st & 25th & 26th 727th R.E. & 103rd M.G Coy in course of construction at PETIT MORTIER — Inspected camps situated at FORT ROMPU — ERQUINGHEM — Visited troops of ERQUINGHEM Mentry Home Defence in district. Visited — Saw Town Major on route infect — Visited Insanitary billet at RUE MARLE —	M7
CROIX DU BAC	23.X.16	1 pm	Sanitary arrangement for emptys (cesspit—Saw Capt SMEDLEY of 102nd Field Ambulance re work being carried out at Clean, Rebuilt manure pits	M7
CROIX DU BAC	24.X.16 — 2.XI.16		On leave. Took over MHD Advance States duties at Return them.	

(Sd) W Stewart Capt RAMC
O.C. 7th Sanitary Section.

WAR – DIARY

of

O/C. 7th. SANITARY SECTION

NOVEMBER – 1916.

VOL. II.

PAGES.

WAR DIARY or INTELLIGENCE SUMMARY

Army Form No. 1

Place	Date	Hour	Summary of Events and Information	Remarks and references to Appendices
CROIX DU BAC	3.XI.16	7.30p	Returned from leave. Resumed duties as ADMS. Visited ERQUINGHEM & near R.A.O. in charge - on RUE MARLE rouchets with some - called FORT ROMPO.	OR.
CROIX DU BAC	4.XI.16	7.30p	Visited ROLANDERIE - L'ARMÉE - CANTEEN FARM - rendezvous with a RUE DELATREE - Paid a visit to ERQUINGHEM received W. for 10th Div. in area - Visited various billets around Pont-ROMPO.	OR.
CROIX DU BAC	5.XI.16	7.30p	Visited HQ of A & B By 152 RFA - saw RMO regarding arrangements re A/152 ATS By 152 RTH & A/By 175 RTH — also Zo 1 Section RAMC rations units.	OR.
CROIX DU BAC	6.XI.16	7.30p	Visited FORT ROMPO - RUE DORMOIRE with ADMS relative sites for field latrines for troops, afterwards proceeded to SALLY Road re shelter further sites & rations, Section of troops RAMC. In afternoon visited a number of RFA units on DOOLIEU Road.	OR.
CROIX DU BAC	7.XI.16	7.30p	Visited D/A B/q Transport lines, A/152 RFA, also Transport lines of C/182 B/q 180, B, C/B/q 175, returning in back areas.	OR.
CROIX DU BAC	8.XI.16	7.30p	Visited Candier, Pont ROMPU with ADMC & Off. CHANCE - Arranged Sanitarian Inspection at Institution et School at Sainthonier. - Visited various Camps on BAC ST MAUR — ERQUINGHEM Road with Sup. Engineer of 4th Corps Sec. rearranging for starting water for filtering plants — in ERQUINGHEM.	OR.
CROIX DU BAC	9.XI.16	7.30p	Visited HQ of A & B Bys 160 BE RFA and interviewed 2 M.O. regarding accomodation for sick in train for A.B/175 - B/RFA. - Visited R.B/160 B/q Transport lines & No3 Section BAC. Transport lines of A/B, C B/q 175 BY. R.F.H. - Went with supervisor rearranging billets of field on CROIX DU BAC - BAC ST MAUR Road. Made informal instruction for public latrine. Visited A.P.M. rearranging hire of hand carts from Sani Sec. St. Venant.	OR.
CROIX DU BAC	10.XI.16	7.30p	Visited A.P.M. (Captain COMBE) - Visited labor yards of sub-sanitary Sect. on BAC ST MAUR - ERQUINGHEM road - noted rapid shortage of carts - sent collecting of Nov 6. to 8. - Saw OC No 4 Sp. Coy in matters. - Visited camps along BAC ST MAUR — ERQUINGHEM Road with Officer of 16 S. Bn. Engineer re water sterilizing plants. Sites for latrines - Rode ERQUINGHEM, NUEVE-EGLISE Road, enquiring for public latrines &others. Visited present as. - Clerks sent for help to latrine ERQUINGHEM, FARMENTIERES, visited 10th RFA. at	OR.

WAR DIARY
or
INTELLIGENCE SUMMARY

Army Form No 2

(Erase heading not required.)

Instructions regarding War Diaries and Intelligence Summaries are contained in F. S. Regs., Part II. and the Staff Manual respectively. Title Pages will be prepared in manuscript.

Place	Date	Hour	Summary of Events and Information	Remarks and references to Appendices
CROIX DU BAC	11.xi.16	6.30pm	ARMENTIERES repairs to roofs & roads for billets; refuge. Visits 2nd & Section of 24th D.C. Markets. Supply of wire for clothes lines. Visited C.R.E's department, reports & return of billets for latrine repairs & labour baths.	O.R.
CROIX DU BAC	12.xi.16	7.30pm	Visits 2nd Section 1st D.T. in disinfector camp. Toilet munitions (blankets) in want of examination — note to ERQUINGHEM now 2nd Army areas. inspect room N.C.O. for work & the 2nd in area — Went with A.D.M.S. Front rented by C B.175 R.F.A. Transport Lines to the Depot.	O.R.
CROIX DU BAC	13.xi.16	7.30pm	Visited billets rented by D B4.175 R.F.A. [illeg]. Main camp of Diphtheria has occurred at ARMENTIERES. Inspected — Rd on 6 RUE MARLE & [illeg] information from 105th British Hosp — Marked a suspicious case of Diphtheria. Visited billet (SPRING FARM) — RUE FLEURIE. Sand arrangement for Disinfection. Visited various camps & area around Engine Farm.	O.R.
CROIX DU BAC	15.xi.16	7.30pm	Inspected a number of well immediately behind Subsidiary line with a view to arranging the supply of drinking water — reports on same to A.D.M.S.	O.R.
CROIX DU BAC	14.xi.16	7.30pm	Visited 101 R.G.C. Transport Lines re numbers of camps on ERQUINGHEM — BAC ST MAUR road. Went to BAILLEUL, returned conferred of Sanitary Officer. Altered water from (Bois) LA ANTRAY officer.	O.R.
CROIX DU BAC	15.xi.16	7.30pm	Visited BOIS GRENIER. Borrow pumps station — also rubbish at WHITE CITY — BIRDCAGE — WATER FARM — SALIENT POST — BURNT FARM. Enquiry to same 6 ADMS. Several public latrines put up. Visited billets at ERQUINGHEM Aug Farm & Scobie Farm re tree shelter from [illeg] D Y's spray storm sand defect for puncture. Wind 5 Marine water supplies re [illeg] — CHARDS FARM LILLE POST.	O.R.
CROIX DU BAC	16.xi.16	7.30pm	PARADISE ALLEY WINB AVENUE & TRAMLINE AVENUE whole town before sending for public latrines on ERQUINGHEM — ARMENTIERES road. Visited camp on BAC ST MAUR — ERQUINGHEM road. Enquiry to weak bone — wire ERQUINGHEM enquiry with — Visited water farm (pumps) station. mentioned O/c — wire to BOIS GRENIER. Enquiry went from a will 6 tanks at RATION FARM.	O.R.

1875 Wt. W593/826 1,000,000 4/15 J.B.C. & A. A.D.S.S./Forms/C. 2118.

Army Form C. 2118

No. 3

WAR DIARY
or
INTELLIGENCE SUMMARY
(Erase heading not required.)

Place	Date	Hour	Summary of Events and Information	Remarks and references to Appendices
CROIX DU BAC	19.XI.16	7.30 p	Visited various Camps on BAC ST MAUR – ERQUINGHEM road re giving ok results. Met Sanitary Section NC in camp nr (first line) – Visited ERQUINGHEM. Tram arrangements marked. Saturation then nc. says [illegible] Officer N.C. Renvoi Bryant Ave. – Called at 102 Field Ambulance. Interviewed Col. IRVINE re arrgts / transport. Future arrangmts with her troops. 2 horses. Saw part of ERQUINGHEM.	OR
CROIX DU BAC	4.XI.16	7.30 p	Routine.	
CROIX DU BAC	20.XI.16	7.30 p	Visited 30 Field Worksp near cutting arrangement Repairs. Two water supply. Saw extract in Battalion [illegible] Orders. [illegible] Fen direction supply [illegible] Maxwell Nelson Clerk for Sup. Bay w/ BACSTMAUR railway station [illegible]	OR
CROIX DU BAC	21.XI.16	7.30 p	[illegible] Section. Visited 30 Field Worksp re visit to Bath supply returns – [illegible] water supply – 103rd Transport [illegible] in course of construction. 221.– 26. [illegible] Sgt. Roy C Field to Sr Ex constitution water.	OR
CROIX DU BAC	22.XI.16	7.30 p	Sup.Co. – Rode (Billet bullion) Composn. ctg Sanitary Officer – [illegible] Inspected Camps of A B & Bn. 160 Bty RFA + A Bn 175 Bty RFA Toronto Camp – 2, 3, 74 Sections. SAC also so [illegible] M.s. Visited ERQUINGHEM re supply or Sanitary and reading reserve arms – also Camps T.Pul Cn.	OR
CROIX DU BAC	23.XI.16	7.30 p	(details on) FORT ROMPU – ERQUINGHEM Road. Visited the Ryan earlier As Pat. in Transport – [illegible] re constitution Officers & NCOs. [illegible] At [illegible] W.Os. separate. Your Sub. Ration [illegible] Hauts. ADMS.	OR
CROIX DU BAC	24.XI.16	7.30 p	Inspected Sub. area cabot death translation to the execution of WHITE CITY– visited K.ADMs. + Regimental Baths. Post – J.F., ack. ADMS – Visited [illegible] of ERQUINGHEM with ADMS– Attended C.R.E. Premiers Sanitary Marcieu with O.C.– Visited 11- Ambt. AT R.56 [illegible]	OR
CROIX DU BAC	25.XI.16	7.30 p	Visited Regnt Coy and Post in Trenches with ADMS also short trench arm. Visited Hqts. 113 A.T. Report carr. of section. Royal Scots at LAROLANDERIE PETITE also huts at – LA GRANDE ROLANDERIE + [illegible] water supply of [illegible] Pay out [illegible] of ERQUINGHEM.	OR
CROIX DU BAC	26.XI.16	7.30 p	(illegible) Trench matters only non- [illegible] Sup. Bay [illegible] Later visited Huts. Set of LA BOUDRELLE+ PETIT MORTIER re pole latrines with inmates of Sup. Bay [illegible] by Informal Inspection – Visited Hqts Nt 34 + 20 C Supply [illegible] [illegible] Inspection touch am. ADDS to the	OR

1875 Wt. W 593/826 1,000,000 4/15 J.B.C. & A. A.D.S.S./Forms/C. 2118.

WAR DIARY
or
INTELLIGENCE SUMMARY
(Erase heading not required.)

Army Form C. 2118.

Place	Date	Hour	Summary of Events and Information	Remarks and references to Appendices
CROIX DU BAC	27.XI.16	7.30p	Visited camp occupied by 11th Bde at T. Coy RE & interviewed O.C. in/c of Camp. Inspected billets — Visited HQ of 16th R. Fus list at ROLANDERIE (Petit) in ref: to water supply — on RUE DES ACQUETS — Visited billets occupied by R.G.A. 155 — Rfty Baaks — Reported Nil.	Apx.
CROIX DU BAC	28.XI.16	7.30p	Visited HQ of 207 (I) R.E. ERQUINGHEM made further enquiries Cesspit — interviewed prior the night interpreter [Tournay] as to cost of sanitary at SHY — a situation in their town unit by troops. — Interview O.C. Recrea Bn — Tournay for [hand] over place our sanitarians further our fit coverage of latrines in yard for night use — On the BOIS GRENIER enquires water supplies in Right Sector & [Trench] reports	Apx.
CROIX DU BAC	29.XI.16	7.30p	On with Son by R.E. Visited shell unexpl: fielded by 25th Bde or Division at Battn heads accompanying in to criticism of latrines in sector re — Or CHAPELLE ARMENTIERES reported with view of all water supplies in Trenches — Reported to ADMS attention especially drawn by Col CHANCE future or Sanitation at Corps in [weather]	Apx.
CROIX DU BAC	30.XI.16	7.30p	Visited Col IRVINE at 102 J.G. r/yard [wiring] Park R.A.A. [Travels] By 2nd II at A.16 & 9-1 Shd 36 — interviewed O.I.C. & arranged for further water supply, this section of Sanitation, in permanent	Apx.

[signature] Captain R.A.M.C.T.
30.XI.16.

34 Div.

140/1943 — Vol 12

SECRET
Dec. 1916.

WAR. DIARY
of
O/c. 74th. SANITARY. SECTION.

DECEMBER 1916.

VOLUME. XII   PAGES. 5.

COMMITTEE FOR THE
MEDICAL HISTORY OF THE WAR
Date   13 MAR. 1917

WAR DIARY
or
INTELLIGENCE SUMMARY
(Erase heading not required.)

Army Form C. 2118

Place	Date	Hour	Summary of Events and Information	Remarks and references to Appendices
CROIX DU BAC	1.XII.16	7.30 p	Visited with DMS camps at FORT ROMPU occupied by 71st, 52nd H.A.G. Shaft Regiment R.G.A. Fort to provision of Batht. recently fully occupied by 25th Divn. Took some by Sanitary Section Man in absence to Corps Instructor at School at ESTAIRES & afterwards visited Transport lines of 24th, 26th, 27th Bns. also of 20th T.B.D. & Tr. at PETIT MORTIER, inspected camp area. W. R. is Coy. A.S.C.	ADS
CROIX DU BAC	2.XII.16	7.30 p	Re Fr. BOIS GRENIER - visited water troughs arrangements for reconstruction. Place from Capt. School of Instruction on Rt. 7th also instructed Town Major ERQUINGHEM, inspected all French Cookhouses in Right Sector with M.O. of occupying Battalion (16th R.S. — 10th Rh. whs) in FORT ROMPU — ERQUINGHEM road — interviewed M.Os. 27th — 27th in FORT ROMPU — ERQUINGHEM & arrangements for bivouacs.	ADS
CROIX DU BAC	3.XII.16	3 p.m	Visited camps occupied by 28th & 27th, 27th 27th 27th in KERQUINGHEM & arrangements for bivouacs. M.O.s inspected certain sanitary arrangements — on KERQUINGHEM road FR. Post on following town.	ADS
CROIX DU BAC	4.XII.16	7.30 p	Visited billet occupied by 26th Bn. in RUE DORMOIRE also billets recently vacated by R.G.A. Howitzers on Rt. Inspected 22 cookhouses in Rt. Sector of Trenches	ADS
CROIX DU BAC	5.XII.16	7.50 p	Visited camps occupied by 26th — 27th 9 R.F.S. also Gillet Nyamdi Section of Sanitary appliances — interview rep. in O.S. Visited Corps School of Instruction in afternoon with A.D.M.S.	ADS
CROIX DU BAC	6.XII.16	7.30 p	Ran return Reconstratops on Sanitation from 9.30 a.m — 12.30 p.m. Re Div. Capt. Instruction at School at ESTAIRES — visited water fault at JESUS FARM — Visited have recently by G.O.C. 34 Division — at CROIX DU BAC & property on Prov- stopped up in water — Visited billets at CHAPPELLE ARMENTIERES (I.D.2.S.) & arrangements necessary &-fitted of French Inspection of Queen — water fault — also visited Section of tr. necessary Sanitary arrangements with Sous Camp Commandant March transport of French from CROIX DU BAC to Pontac (lyghts) at LA BOUDRELLE & BAC ST MAUR (for trains for use)	ADS

WAR DIARY or INTELLIGENCE SUMMARY

Army Form C. 2118

Place	Date	Hour	Summary of Events and Information	Remarks and references to Appendices
CROIX DU BAC	7.XII.16	7.45 a.m.	Visited Baths, Water Supply at JESUS FARM with class of In Os from Cooks Instructional School ESTAIRES – Called on Camp Commandant to transport of 17th Lanc Regt & Camp standing with HQ 2nd ERQUINGHEM repair Sanitary action as at HQ ERQUINGHEM repair Sanitary action instructions. Vr 29 R.F. [public latrines, highly interesting] Vr 27 R.F.	a/r
CROIX DU BAC	8.XII.16	7.30 a.m.	Visited Camp occupied by 27 R.F. C Coy on BAC ST MAUR – ERQUINGHEM road – fairly [sat.] in course of erection – Visited billets occupied by 23rd Th.B. in RUE DELATREE in/which are required (photo) huts – Pan instruction, small rooms – water fair, stairs & chairs at purchase, latrine new built, for an – Visited 10th M.G.C. who had camps by 10 & shared by B B/y 152 & R.F. & Louster Farm (occupied by twenty Bn of Th B (sick), 1st HQ 152nd Bs RFA in RUE DELATREE much encampment by that supply. water.	a/r
CROIX DU BAC	9.XII.16	4 p.m.	Visited Camp occupied by 2/FC on CROIX DU BAC ~ ERQUINGHEM road when to inform RCO of matter of occupation of public latrines – lightly unsatisfactory but in course of alteration as (CROIX DU BAC with a large movement supply, 17 in offensive supply with HQ of Sanitary water assessment for Camp – well sworn with some water.	a/t
CROIX DU BAC	10.XII.16	7 p.m.	Visited ERQUINGHEM throughout public incineration with [illegible] situation – would wish to rest Capt PARKIN Sanitary fficer – inspected flow all water supplies RUE DU BIEZ south of Rue.	a/t
CROIX DU BAC	11.XII.16 7.30p		Visited all 16th Tramas in RUE DELATREE thorn junction of RUE DU BIEZ & RUE DE TROIS TOULETTES particularly water supply & latrines – (or 4 new) – for authorizing source.	a/r
CROIX DU BAC	12.XII.16	7.30 p.m.	Visited billets in Course of construction in [illegible] & R side of ERQUINGHEM - ARMENTIERES R travelled on interior walk Ct. Lieut Fry of Sanitary Labastre – [illegible] (RMy water supply in RUE DES AGUETTES – GRIS POT – L'ARNEE & RUE DELATREE.	a/r

Army Form C. 2118

WAR DIARY
or
INTELLIGENCE SUMMARY
(Erase heading not required.)

Instructions regarding War Diaries and Intelligence Summaries are contained in F. S. Regs., Part II. and the Staff Manual respectively. Title Pages will be prepared in manuscript.

3

Place	Date	Hour	Summary of Events and Information	Remarks and references to Appendices
CROIX DU BAC	19.xii.16	7.30 p.m	Visited a number of billets occupied by reinforcement of 15th & 16th Royal Scots — sent party from Sanitary Section to put billets into a sanitary condition — Visited B. By. transport billets occupied by the 16th Royal Scots. An improvement was noted at LA BECQUE & present area — 9.i.w DOULIEU	Capt.
CROIX DU BAC	14.xii.16	6 p.m	Visited billets occupied by reinforcement for 15th Suffolks at NOOTE BOOM interviewed O.L.C. in command — for billets — R.P. put in to Sanitary Condition — Rota on & BAILLEUL	Capt.
CROIX DU BAC	15.xii.16	7 p.m	Visited Hqrs & 11th Suffolks at LA ROLANDERIE PETITE also L'ARMEE 770 & 15th R.W. Scot in RUE DELPIERRE. In afternoon went to NOOTE BOOM re-visited a number of billets occupied by Reinforcement — 16 Suffs – 2 deficiencies noted	Capt.
CROIX DU BAC	16.xii.16	7.30 p.m	Gen Victor Production on Sanitation at Corps Instruction of Schools ESTAIRES from 9.30 a.m to 12.30 p.m Remainder of afternoon with fellow instruction of D.M.S. Provision of Schl & Inoculation for Troops — R.M. ERQUINGHEM was deficient — To 1 Sanitation of Sanitary Duties	Capt.
CROIX DU BAC	17.xii.16	7 p.m	Visited billets occupied by 20th Northumberland Fusiliers, also Wks. under Division at Battn. of Letter of Sanitation with 1st Co. Scott construction at S.W. corner of Battn & A.D.M.S. 34th Division at Battn re putting situation with D.M at LA BECQUE BH. & 16th Royal Scots at LA BECQUE for some time billets newly occupied by 150 reinforcement to 16th Suffs. with furniture transport — Called to by Off. with. billets are dirty by 150 reinforcement of Chaplain — drinking water deficient to Sanitary Inspector of Suff — R.ing by A.D.M.S. — Sanitary with him, enquired into fill	Capt.
CROIX DU BAC	18.xii.16	7 p.m	Inspected A. & B. By. 160 R.F.A. Transport — Ruin of Suff. & arranged — Rgt. TONSON RYE one with new Sanitary Inspector of Suff.	Capt.
CROIX DU BAC	19.xii.16	7 p.m	Visited billets occupied by 20ths N.F. at E. end of Division at Battn — ERQUINGHEM Visited new Rifle Range at FORT ROMPU & ERQUINGHEM Through agreement for civilian labour. All men train for heavy fatigue Infantry Transport Lines 11/F.A. 21 & 152 R.F.A.	Capt.

1875 Wt. W593/826 1,000,000 4/15 J.B.C. & A. A.D.S.S./Forms/C. 2118.

WAR DIARY
or
INTELLIGENCE SUMMARY
(Erase heading not required.)

Army Form C. 2118

Place	Date	Hour	Summary of Events and Information	Remarks and references to Appendices
CROIX DU BAC	20.XII.16	7.15 p.m.	Visited camps on FORT ROMPU — ERQUINGHEM road and ADMS 61st Division visited BEF Canteen & YMCA HUT at BAC ST MAUR — rest hydrantte. visited O.C. Sanitary Section of 51st Division — NEW ZEALAND Division at SAILLY — inspected their main Sanitary fatigue Villa — New Zealand Division at BAC ST MAUR — arrangement for their Sanitary fatigue Villa —	ADMS
CROIX DU BAC	21.XII.16	7 p.m.	Visited ERQUINGHEM — Interviewed Senior R.C.O. of Sanitary Section interior Sanitary matters — Visited billets occupied by C Coy 21st Northumberland Fusiliers in the East side of RUE DORMOIRE — attended Sanitary matters	ADMS
CROIX DU BAC	22.XII.16	6 p.m.	In Orderly Room. Visited various billets at RUE MARLE L'ARMEE with R.C.O. in change — made arrangements for erection of public latrines etc. at RUE MARLE	ADMS
CROIX DU BAC	23.XII.16	7 p.m.	Went from BILLETS S.W. of Division and Back. ERQUINGHEM Inter R.C.O.s in of Sanitary Section & T.V. attached — Inspected latrines, incinerators in Italian traps in new area.	ADMS
CROIX DU BAC	24.XII.16	4 p.m.	Visited the R.A.P. of Division "Battn" at ERQUINGHEM — Investigated work done by Sanitary Section — visited H.Q. of 27 North umb(erland) Fusiliers (1st line) reserve to filled in the trenches — also inspected billets at S.E. end of town at Battn. in field H.Q. Brigade H.Q. at ERQUINGHEM Permitted — required 15th 102 Brigade to fill up by 10th BS on 23.XII.16 reported to A.D.M.S. on arrangements made — signed Wills to B. & Wilson —	ADMS C.O.
CROIX DU BAC	25.XII.16	1 p.m.	Carried out inspection with fellow officer at Sans-See Mgr with reports to commanding officer of each to attend to small things	O.C.
CROIX DU BAC	26.XII.16	7.30 p.m.	matter of 10 July Room — Visited ERQUINGHEM with R.C.O. in change - to visited New hospital School preparing for the purpose — went contact of Captain Mr Mr Mr Mr R.C.O. Society of & infected at R.C.O. Mission — Visited after-care - Visited Casualty in patients in B. Rivers Brigade hour — O.C. Pioneer Brigade area — Visited Stretcher bearer 6 horse Ambulance — investigated & approved rechecked — the 6 horse Ambulance in the purpose - with a day's consultation at ERQUINGHEM — interviewed Ma Captain (Captain COLT-WILLIAMS) cont. on all his & 108 Brigade H.Q.s. — ERQUINGHEM to visited & inspected the new of Sanitary School — Included A.D.S. on inter-inspection etc. etc. — Visited 102 Surg Stat - Inspected — Visited SWIN BORN - today after visit followed — with in consultation — Visit ADM. Salt Button Hospital H.Q. Brigade Division Corps — CROIX DU BAC — BAC ST MAUR road inspected full-orchestral by Officer of BAC ST MAUR High Road in Inf, (Sig) if the much better now — HS with & A.P.M. inf/arty Transport Officer of 101st A.D.C. Marles & their new stored constit — in A.D.M.S.	ADMS

1875 Wt. W 593/826 1,000,000 4/15 J.B.C. & A. A.D.S.S./Forms/C. 2118.

Army Form C. 2118

WAR DIARY or INTELLIGENCE SUMMARY

Place	Date	Hour	Summary of Events and Information	Remarks and references to Appendices
Croix du Bac	27.XII.16	4 p.m.	Rode to Corps Institution at School at ESTAIRES & heard lecture by Major MILMAN for new School of Instruction (Divisional) for O.R. — then in conjunction with Lt-Colonel IRVINE DC. 102 ADMS 34th Division attended for full Adjudant - subjects [illegible] our own unit by Major accompany with his instructor - Put up [illegible] for a small pull-over institutional uniform [illegible] (Private or Corps School, & later on Pilot Unit) ADMS 34th Division.	OK
Croix du Bac	28.XII.16	7 p.m.	RUE DORMOIRE & interviewed 2 O.C. Scottish Rifles in made return of billet occupied by Col. in HERQUINGHEM then Coy. N.C.O. & men - RUE DORMOIRE & RUE DU MOULIN then traveled by 16th Northumberland Fusiliers Section all Saturday arrangement - visit of RE Hospital (Infectious) [illegible] —	W/Z
Croix du Bac	30.XII.16	7.30 a.m.	Visited BOIS GRENIER - WHITE CITY - BIRDCAGE - WATER FARM - TRAMLINE AVENUE. BURNT FARM - RATION FARM - WINDY GATES now built in Trenchwork inspection in their condition as made. Work done RE: & ADMS 34.	W/Z
Croix du Bac	30.XII.16	7.30 a.m.	Visited ARMENTIERES Baths and Village - Many ERQUINGHEM Baths Subscription TO's Division - Interviewed successor [illegible] at ablative Rode & efficient RUE MARLE & interviewed Second in command of 2/1st A.C.B. write head of Sanitary arrangement, [illegible] way in other District.	OK
Croix du Bac	31.XII.16	4.30 p.m.	Visited Water Supply in Rifle Sch. ADMS 34th Division - Interviewed Officer RC & repaired field oven referred him deficient carried out by Sanitary Section with own cart.	OK

(T) Stewart Capt. RAMC.

34th Div.

140/1917 Vol 13

War Diary
of
o/c 7th. Sanitary Section

January 1917

Vol XIII   Pages. 5.

SECRET
Jan 1917

COMMITTEE FOR THE
MEDICAL HISTORY OF THE WAR
Date 13 MAR. 1917

WAR DIARY or INTELLIGENCE SUMMARY

Army Form C. 2118

(Erase heading not required.)

Place	Date	Hour	Summary of Events and Information	Remarks and references to Appendices
CROIX DU BAC	1.1.17	7.30 p.m.	Gave lecture on Sanitation at Corps Instructional School at ESTAIRES from 9.30 a.m. – 12.30 p.m. (ADMS visited). ERQUINGHEM Tablet in shed near Divisional Baths which has been [unclear].	ADS.
CROIX DU BAC	2.1.17	7.30 p.m.	Visited billet at NOOTE BOOM occupied by [unclear] for [unclear] 2nd 8 Regt – interview O.C. & instructed Sect. of Sanitary Section to carry out [unclear] construction, Returned Sanitary arrangements in billets – water supply – billet interviewed O.C. 10th Gloucesters – Reported to ADMS. Visited V.D. Hospital treatment instructing Captn. TAGGART meaning arrangements for sites. Sanitary Reports in detail. Fort Romper – [unclear] Captn. TAGGART meaning arrangements for new kitchen at Sanitary School.	ADS.
CROIX DU BAC	3.1.17	7.30 p.m.	Visited the Sanitary School at FORT ROMPO with Captn. TAGGART. Ian [unclear] the Sanitation at the V.D. Hospital at Robak – met Captn. [unclear] (Adml.) at ESTAIRES – interviewed.	ADS.
CROIX DU BAC	4.1.17	4 p.m.	Col. IRVINE – R.A.M.C. A.D.M.S. 34th Divn. Mounted Staff of LA BOUDRELLE. Inspected [unclear] Scarlet fever at farm. Major Division Instructional Staff at ERQUINGHEM. Royal reception [unclear]. Results of Sanitary School Work – Nature of Sanitary School Inspection [unclear] and of 13th Bn Royal Scots [unclear]. Cars of a battle [unclear] camp – East of RUE DARMOIRES visited instruction at School. Interviewed O.C. Divnl. WARDEN – Inspected outside of battle [unclear]. Tour by farm – about [unclear]. Farm [unclear] inside of [unclear] – Visited R A HdQ at CROIX DU BAC. Reviewed constructions done by Sanitary Section.	ADS.
CROIX DU BAC	6.1.17	7.30 p.m.	Route through Sanitary School at FORT ROMPO with 2nd Lieut minor construction and improvements. Captn. TAGGART – ERQUINGHEM instructional Staff. 2nd STEWART. O/c Hundred School House. Interviewed about [unclear] construction of work. Rode ESTAIRES & NEUE BERQUIN for shewed interest that the construction of baths & [unclear] ADMS.	ADS.
CROIX DU BAC	7.1.17		Visited [unclear] Station at NOOTE BOOM occupied by [unclear] Scottish for 25th Div. 9.17.20 at [unclear] to 5.17 p.m. with A.D. Veterinary.	ADS.

1875. Wt. W593/826 1,000,000 4/15 J.B.C. & A. A.D.S.S./Forms/C. 2118.

Army Form C. 2118

WAR DIARY
or
INTELLIGENCE SUMMARY
(Erase heading not required.)

Place	Date	Hour	Summary of Events and Information	Remarks and references to Appendices
CROIX DU BAC	8.1.17	7 p.m.	Visited Divisional Sanitary School at FORT ROMPU and visited work fire stove by Sanitary men from various units — also to 2nd Bn S.G. Corps (Scottish) saw Major THOMPSON hair/WC School talked to him — Gave lecture on Sanitation. Reported to ADMS.	ADS
CROIX DU BAC	9.1.17	7.30 p.m.	Visited Division Sanitary School at FORT ROMPU —	RAY
			Visited lectures on various insects mosquitos incinerator — saw Lt GRAINGER ERQUINGHEM — Visited hospital school gave instruction on cantonment — Visited camp at FORT ROMPU group of STEWART OIL, Sanitary School on Right Bank, Visited various Sanitary School places in area then visited Sanitation.	DSS
CROIX DU BAC	10.1.17	7.30 p.m.	Loto 2 jobs with the R.O. Visited various in use. CROIX DU BAC — ESTAIRES new place Items Football & Gyms & Toys L.V.S. photo on ADMS — Visited Divisional Sanitary School Van Loton on Sanitation	DSS
CROIX DU BAC	11.1.17	7.30 p.m.	Visited Division of instruction School gave lecture on work — To ERQUINGHEM May Survey & C.O. III on Santh team cement — Visited Divisional Sanitary School — afterwards Van Loton on Sanitation.	WS
CROIX DU BAC	12.1.17	7.30 p.m.	Gave lecture at Corps School of Instruction — ESTAIRES on Sanitation — lecture on Sanitation at lectures at Sanitary School at FORT ROMPU from 9.30 a.m. — 12.30 p.m. — Gave last first 5 days course of instruction of Divisional Sanitary School completed — Rtd ERQUINGHEM May Cardinal — Was attended Saturday	DSS
CROIX DU BAC	13.1.17	7.30 p.m.	ADMS 34 Brigade IRVINE-hospital in St NOOTE BOOM fell on lintel Nod — with duties: ADMS 34 Brigade IRVINE-hospital in St NOOTE BOOM fell on lintel went into RUE MARLE with Da DMS of 34th Div. lyte BALLINGALL DR. by him Visited a number of billets in engineer of Buer & Oxford & CROIX DU BAC mostly with Daly Visited billets occupied by Grand & 90 mm. After 2.1 new Ratifying Inquiry arrived 2.30 R.A.'s supply ADMS on various Sanitary construction — Visited billet created by the occupant. Met shortly, rightly & on right bank of STEENWERCK — Saw Captain WILSON at Officium Hospital — Made Supply on Visiting Sanitary arrangements of Russia & administration corps team — R.H.Q. Hand books of 2 R.F.A. first experiments by Special A.F.B.H. 100 F.E. R.F.A. or & Hal in 3 butteries at punter of STURT ADS	ADS
CROIX DU BAC	15.1.17	1 p.m.	Visited A.P.M. Trade arrangement & Gr May Felium out a Tramlin but billets — on to Divisional Sanitary School Ins Visited back Gas Post by class on ERQUINGHEM — Visited batters centre built for Gas School — water supply on TRAMLINE AVENUE — then ADMS — Visited HQ & 307 Fd.Coy R.E. at ERQUINGHEM ranking a can	ADS

1875 Wt. W593/826 1,000,000 4/15 J.B.C. & A. A.D.S.S./Forms/C. 2118.

WAR DIARY
or
INTELLIGENCE SUMMARY

Army Form C. 2118

3

Place	Date	Hour	Summary of Events and Information	Remarks and references to Appendices
CROIX DU BAC	16.1.17	9 pm	Inspected billets that accommodate for disinfection. Conference with divisional Sanitary Sect. R.E.'s with O.C. 103rd Field Ambulance — for the purpose of the 18th & 26th Rode to FORT ROMPU to discuss Latrine Funnels under supervision of Sanitary Sect. Men to train as Sanitarians — Class ended Lecture under supervision of Sanitary Officer	M.T.
CROIX DU BAC	17.1.17	7.30pm	Visited Divisional Sanitary School at FORT ROMPU — inspected camp occupied by 21st R.F. & 2 Sany R.E. Co. & Sanitary Section. FORT ROMPU with R.O. (Lt WHITESIDE) (Lt) Col CHANCE (D.S.O.) our Return on Sanitation at Brigade Sanitary School — Interviewed Col CHANCE Q. & A. & 31st Brigade Trans. for Water Supply over the crater in Camp & billets. Typ. applied by 102nd Field Ambulance.	M.T.
CROIX DU BAC	19.1.17	9 pm	Visited Divisional Sanitary School at FORT ROMPU — inspected latrines — inspected camp occupied by 2nd R.F. at FORT ROMPU — Sanitary Squad DAVIES of 7th Sanitary Section in absence of N.C.O. Sanitary School	M.T.
CROIX DU BAC	19.1.17	7.30 pm	2326 o/o Staff Sgt HENDERSON. S.I. posted to Cavalry Station on arrival — Divisional Sanitary School inspected today. Received instructions from Sqd Kelmann DAVIES of 7th San Sy — Rode GERDOINGHEM inspected Field Oven & went over on wire direction by 2/Lt DAVIES R.G.A today & visited Horse lines, Army Service Corps FORT ROMPU — went on inside the towns building. Our visit at Divl Sanitary Sch.	M.T.
CROIX DU BAC	20.1.17	7 pm	Visited HQ N 152 Brigade R.F.a. major of & 2 officers reported sick with Jaundice — advised Rd. hosp to fever — field sprayed out — On BOIS GRENIER visit watersupply at CROM BALDT FARM — BIRDCAGE — WATER FARM — TRAMLINE AVENUE — RATION FARM & WINDY GATES FARM inspected	M.T.
CROIX DU BAC	21.1.17	7 pm	Inspected water supply & arrangements — Salt Scales — Manu ad — Complete inspection of all supplies to Brandrum — reports on hut to ADMS reads with O.C.R.E	M.T.

WAR DIARY
or
INTELLIGENCE SUMMARY

Army Form C. 2118

Place	Date	Hour	Summary of Events and Information	Remarks and references to Appendices
CROIX DU BAC	22.1.17	7 pm	Visited Divisional Sanitary School received work in progress — on camp at FORT ROMPU in afternoon. Camp occupied by 21st R. Fus. – for STEENWERCK — Major O.C. 16th Supply Column regrets loss of shelter. Riquic. – Visited Divisional Sanitary School of Service. – Divisional Sanitary School was visited by D.D.M.S. of 2nd ANZAC CORPS – The third class of Sanitary N.C.O's was commencing today.	WR
CROIX DU BAC	23.1.17	4 pm	Gun (shown on Sanitation to class of N.C.O's at Corps School Instruction at ESTAIRES from 9.30 am – 12.30 pm – Visited Divisional Sanitary School & then returned to CROSTRUM.	WR
CROIX DU BAC	24.1.17	7 pm	Infantry Farm town at LA BOUDRELLE war card Seaward Town before MONT — went to CHAPELLE ARMENTIÈRES regt — (A. Car of Sus pm to O.S.F. MONT) — visited Field — Surveys of troops ERQUINGHEM Visited Divisional Sanitary School Man Lecture.	WR
CROIX DU BAC	25.1.17	7 pm	Visited ERQUINGHEM + interviewed O/c Rescue Billets their travels. Inspected & entered on your system for troops. Conference to them hospitalities — Interviewing the write-sham Institutional (sanitary School + appurtenances.	WR
CROIX DU BAC	26.1.17	7 pm	Rescue Order Inspector to above — visited Divisional Sanitary School. Went to ruins on back of units — at the Subordinate Tubes has ERQUINGHEM there are all arrangements for troops, as no bous return.	WR
FLETRE	27.1.17	7 pm	System truly from W 6.15 am. — Starred at 9.30 a.m. with D.D.G. among FLETRE 10.25 am. RD. ARMENTIÈRES to ERQUINGHEM – Settling of outlook accompt for Villages + Civilian (colour interviewing O.C. Sand Section — New Project twining — also TATI S. (s.) Institution hospital. After going Sir Arthur with A.D.M.S. 3rd Australian Division — difficulty of any arrangement of CROIX DU BAC in charge of this N.C.O. during FLETRE at 2.30 pm for greater than sufficient operation of the War nothing in Inspection + Sanitary arrangements of short form to CROIX DU BAC for one night.	WR
FLETRE	28.1.17	7 pm	Carried out Cutting Supply am — Interview with FLETRE in afternoon — also + & units of Sanitary of Sanitary School — HAZEBROCK.	WR

WAR DIARY or INTELLIGENCE SUMMARY

Army Form C. 2118

Place	Date	Hour	Summary of Events and Information	Remarks and references to Appendices
FLETRE	29.1.17	7 p	Visited with ADMS the HQ. of 104th Pct at COURTE CROIX, of 103rd Pct at BERTHEN road & at CAESTRE also Cavalry Division at Battn & 9th Corps Baths Informant re H.Q. the Division - found them completing forms up - number of Section invalids to Division unit in District.	ADS.
FLETRE	30.1.17	7.30 pm	Visited METEREN & COURTE CROIX road in reconnaissance District - 9th & 15th Corps Instructional School at ESTAIRES, the two way Col. MURRAY saw department of R.E. pumps thence to above baths Indent - 9th Corps - Cavalry Corps with a view to three being made by 3rd Army.	ADS.
FLETRE	31.1.17	7.30 pm	Paid several visits to 9th Corps Cavalry Corps Battn - parties for Sanitary Section employed pushing up showy baths within - Risk of Sanitary Section employed in inspection of billets in Division of area re Fletre Cleaner baths from CROIX DU BAC.	ADS.

W Broward Capt. R.A.M.C.T.

O/c 74th SANITARY SECTION.

34th Div.

WAR DIARY
of
O/c 7th Sanitary Section
for
FEBRUARY 1917

Volume XIV

WAR DIARY or INTELLIGENCE SUMMARY

Army Form C. 2118

Place	Date	Hour	Summary of Events and Information	Remarks and references to Appendices
FLETRE	1.11.17	7 p.m.	Enquired all day at 9th Corps Battn & Cavalry Corps. Battn, where number of Sanitary Sections were situated. Show Battn. Visited these Battns with A.D.M.S. & afterwards in afternoon. The Cavalry Corps battn were working at 2 p.m. Visited HQ2 of 20th R.H. at THIEUSHOUK & unit which filled recently occupied by a Corporal, who had been sent away with Septicaemia. Officer's mess Sanitary reported to A.D.M.S.	W.S.
FLETRE	2.11.17	10 a.m.	Saw nurse. Visited 9th Corps Battn, Cavalry Corps Battn & South of METEREN. If known factors 9th Corps – Visited Corps Battn at 8 p.m. afterwards from METEREN returning (via ...) part pipe-lines. Went to laundry work in Flanders bay – in (...) Mousseau Farm up for Beer allowances at 11 p.m. in Flanders bay.	W.S.
FLETRE	3.11.17	9 p.m.	Visited Battn round town, made arrangements for supplies of water. Visited HQ2 21st R.H. – Visited 20th R.H.	W.S.
FLETRE	4.11.17	9 p.m.	Went can sulphide disinfectors. Adving for ... shelter – Visited 102 R.E. night (...) Collected dirty clothes from DIV (Sec) Train Battn also from 9th Corps Battn – sorted out to such BOULOGNE	W.S.
FLETRE	5.11.17	7.40 p.m.	Early Inspections in lorry for wash late of – Visited Field Amby received fr. 10th & 8th (9/M) 10th A.C. 101st TMB. M.T.Boi. 18th Royal Soft. Inspection area Baix. Machine of Amby (C. 3 men) went mainly Ry Shoopfeld QMRC ... Paul STRAZEELE. Had fit mid up at 9th R.H. Battn (Cavalry Corps). 5 men bonds with by 15 Royal Scott Morning.	W.S.
FLETRE	6.11.17	9 p.m.	Visited Billets recently vacated by 15 (? RIdes.) 16th Royal Scott -- by 15 R. Scott reports on their unit. A.D.M.S. fitted a linn. 3 and food breads for 2 R.C. Rgt at STRAZEELE. Carried 3 old batts to find about Workshop at HAZEBROUCK. Though took such for battn in laundry.	W.S.

Army Form C. 2118

WAR DIARY
or
INTELLIGENCE SUMMARY
(Erase heading not required.)

Place	Date	Hour	Summary of Events and Information	Remarks and references to Appendices
FLETRE	7.ii.17	7h	Visit HQrs of 75th Royal Scots. HQrs transferred by various conveyances – Visit HQrs of 76th Royal Scots midtuesnard	W.S.
FLETRE	8.ii.17	7h	Visit various billets occupied by 10th & 12th cyclers in neighbourhood of MONT DES CATS – also 104th field ambulance – Long enquiry conversation with CO 2nd Batt – Batt at CAESTRE	W.S.
FLETRE	9.ii.17	7h	Visit billets again occupied (billets empty) and transport vehicles transferred cars of various ADMD mrsermt. Nicholson & b. – billets visit billets empty by 11th Suffolks. F20 – RFC motorvans a.v. at Hutterdamn	W.S.
FLETRE	10.ii.17	7h	Visit various conveys – War office visit later (with dp cps) then (later) Batt HQ CAESTRE by train – VT25 & 28th RSH a (BODEWAELSWELDE + 51 P12 – P7 at BARTENACRE) interviewd – their representative at various (Visit Ha) 10thRSH (Halb) BERGUINGHEM	W.S.
FLETRE	11.ii.17	7.15h	Ret to EPERLECQUES. Visit HQ "103rd", HQ "BB" to HQ of 103rd RS returning O.C. (Lt. Col. PHILLIPS) reto HQ mmw Batt at HOUILLE & BAVENGHEM + visit HQ "4 of 26th + 27th RFC returnard representative a.v. convey. Visit HQ of 24th RSM.	W.S.
FLETRE	12.ii.17	7h	Visit billets occupied by 11th Suffolks – 10 Nichol – 15th. 70th Royal Scots interviewed, a.v. of their reliever.	W.S.
FLETRE	13.ii.17	7h	Visit various billets at CAESTRE occupied by 102nd & b.f.C. returnard O.C. reports /vin Sandy and various also visit 206 (O.R.S. new FLETRE)	W.S.
FLETRE	14.ii.17	7h	Visit 15th Supply Column also 206 (O.R.S. – Visit HQrs of 21st – 22nd + 23rd 9th RFC – Visit Hq2 at CAESTRE also 206 (O.R.S. returnard rep. a.v. visit 9th Bath)	W.S.
FLETRE	15.ii.17	7.30h	Ret CAESTRE – returnard O.C. 16th Supply Column – reports + Major Hammond Lawn – O. btbt. Visit vet returnard O.C. m. Wilkie in rest station. Transport a.v. – Visit 104 field Battery + RSF Pron Slow Fult – W.S. returnard for a weres.	W.S.

1875 Wt. W593/826 1,000,000 4/15 J.B.C. & A. A.D.S.S./Forms/C. 2118.

WAR DIARY
or
INTELLIGENCE SUMMARY
(Erase heading not required.)

Army Form C. 2118

Place	Date	Hour	Summary of Events and Information	Remarks and references to Appendices
FLETRE	16.iii.17	7.30 p.	R[?] to AUBIGNY - [?] MDS. 1st Corps - English bath at SAVY TINCQUES MAGNICOURT to ROCOURT & HERMAVILLE afterwards. Visit by laundry (only) at ST MICHEL & filled at DIEVAL when [?] of sanitary section had [?] pay etc. [?]	ADS
FLETRE	17.iii.17	7.30 p.	[?] with ADMS 3rd Division. 6 EPERLECQUES - visit all MDs [?] by 27th Q.[?] in conference with O.C. (McIl.TEMPLE) at BAYENGHEM - [?] to PADs	ADS
FLETRE	18.iii.17	7 p.m.	Visit [?] Suffolks & 10th [?] when ordered by A.D.M.S.	QR
FLETRE→ HERMAVILLE	19.iii.17	7 p.m.	102nd Bde HQ. 1st Bde R.F.A. reports this A.D.M.S. [moved] HQ. 1. The Sanitary Section to HERMAVILLE	QR
HERMAVILLE	20.iii.17	7 p.m.	Visit DIEVAL [?] baths before well flush [?] swell [?] now - on to ROCOURT [?] - interviewed DADOS 1st Div at CHELERS [?]	QR
HERMAVILLE	21.iii.17	7.30 p.m.	[?] ADS [?] [?] baths at CHELERS. Visit bath at HERMAVILLE training filled in villages - [?] with ADMS & CHELERS. MAGNICOURT & ROCOURT also to Corps baths at SAVY.	QR
HERMAVILLE	22.iii.17	7.30 p.	Visit [?] MDS filled in HERMAVILLE [?] water Supplies Rd CHELERS MONCHY-BRETON. LA THIEULOYE - MAGNICOURT ROCOURT & DIEVAL. [?] in church at ROCOURT [?] bath at [?] DADOS 3rd Div - OC Field Amb. at [?]	ADS
HERMAVILLE	23.iii.17	7.30 p.	Visit [?] [?] caught at ECOIVRE [?] 21.iii.17 2 & 93 in [?] Camp Commandant [?] guilty hands with him - also interviewed [?] M.Os - On to ETRUN [?]	ADS

Army Form C. 2118

WAR DIARY
or
INTELLIGENCE SUMMARY
(Erase heading not required.)

Place	Date	Hour	Summary of Events and Information	Remarks and references to Appendices
HERMAVILLE	24.ii.17	7.30 pm	ADMS (qth Div) present. Sanitary arrangement & water supplies discussed at length – on FOR Es officer (qth Div) returned report water supplies in trenches also called at HQ" of qth Div Sanitary Section – on to ST NICHOLAS to view Pumping Station & ST CATHERINE's call. HQ" of 16th R.Fs saw Col SHAKESPEARE re-arrangement of pumping plant needed in area occupied by 51st Division at both – visited Q Bn – Baths at ANZIN.	M.S.
HERMAVILLE	25.ii.17		Ran to ST CATHERINES met with Col SHAKESPEARE. Ran all the trench area occupied by 51st Division. Examined water supplies & sanitary arrangements.	M.S.
HERMAVILLE	25.ii.17	7.30 pm	Visited Trenches. Examined fully the divisional water supplies with Captain STOCK (RE) 22nd R.Fs in front area of 21st & 22nd R.Fs & RONCOURT – Inspected various billets in ST CATHERINES & interviewed Town Majors. With ADMS, saw the OC of 21st & 22nd R.Fs in front area in RONCOURT – Inspected various billets in ST CATHERINES & interviewed Town Majors.	M.S.
HERMAVILLE	26.ii.17	7.30 pm	Visited CHELERS – LATHUILOYE – DIEVAL – BOURS – VAL HUON with ADMS (qth Div) billets interviewed Town Majors.	M.S.
HERMAVILLE	27.ii.17	7.30 pm	Visited HAUTES AVESNES town & Col BIRD – OC 104th Field Ambulance, hospital, & number of sanitary section units – So on to ST POL – ARRAS road for Capt. Latham – visited BETHONSART saw M.O. of 20th R.Fs re military Sanitary Section in his area. Water supply. etc – visited VILLERS BRULIN – saw OC 103rd Field Ambulance & members of his unit. Army course going on in San Sec. te DIEVAL – BETHONSART – HAUTE AVESNES – ST CATHERINE visited ST CATHERINE ST NICHOLAS & investigated water supplies inspected billets & area generally – saw Town Major of ST CATHERINE & Pumps at ville – ??? this area.	M.S.

C.B. Strawbridge Capt R.A.M.C.
O/C 74th SANITARY SECTION

SEC'T
Mar. 1917

140/2043
Vol 45

War Diary
of
96 th. Sanitary Section
for
March 1917

Paper 6.

Vol. 2.

No 15.

COMMITTEE FOR THE
MEDICAL HISTORY OF THE WAR
Date 11 MAY 1917

74th SANITARY SECTION
21/2

Army Form C. 2118

WAR DIARY
or
INTELLIGENCE SUMMARY
(Erase heading not required.)

No 1

Place	Date	Hour	Summary of Events and Information	Remarks and references to Appendices
HERMAVILLE	1.iii.17	7.45 p.m.	Visited ST CATHERINE & ST NICOLAS – to dictate letter arranging with Senior R.C.O. in charge of Sanitary Squad entrusted him in each of these — and visited waterworks [illegible] Staff in attention to R.C.O. in charge of water supplies. Interviewed Town Major of both places. [illegible]	A/3.
HERMAVILLE	2.iii.17	7.30 p.m.	NICOLAS thoroughly inspected their area with Town Major of them all. Visited LATHIELOYE – inspected billets occupied by 1st Royal Scots saw R.B.O [illegible] various Sanitary matters with him – on to DIEVAL – inspected billets [illegible] area with Town R.C.O. in charge of Sanitary instruction [illegible] — Saw [illegible] Staff for public latrines remand.	A/3.
HERMAVILLE	3.iii.17	7.30 p.m.	Interviewed Town Major of HERMAVILLE newly [illegible] public latrines, [illegible] area — also settled with [illegible] provision of public latrines here at. Visited BETHONSART re public work at being on ST POL – ARRAS road. [illegible] R.A.P. [illegible]	A/3.
HERMAVILLE	4.iii.17	7.30 p.m.	Visited TILLOY returned O.C. 16th Supply Column – ST CHELERS Mess Town Major [illegible] arrangements areas with him – made arrangement with so for Trans for supplies coal for huts [illegible] to huts. Visited ROCOURT on MATHIELOYE Turnpike [illegible] billets occupied 15th Royal Scots Returning Q.M.O. – interviewed O.C. 230 Coy A.S.C. on to DIEVAL Met Col. IRVINE of 103rd Brigade arrangements for his huts – Billet grinder by car Panville – Rue [illegible] – Visited Hut Bath at ROCOURT & on to MAGNICOURT [illegible] R.A.P. No. Section.	A/3.
HERMAVILLES.	5.iii.17	7.30 p.m.	Visited ST CATHERINES & ST NICHOLAS in both places re Saw for Paths Major [illegible] for purification. Visited ST AUBIN & LOUEZ re [illegible] TOWN MAJOR.	A/3.
HERMAVILLE	6.iii.17	7.30 p.m.	Visited [illegible] recently built with addition in their water supplies to Sanitary arrangements – also [illegible] at ST NICHOLAS & ST CATHERINE.	A/3.
HERMAVILLE	7.iii.17	7 p.m.	Visited VILLERS BRULIN – GUESTREVILLE & BETHONSART re re a number of billets in turn with O.C. 103rd & Pro. of 34th Div.	A/3.

WAR DIARY
or
INTELLIGENCE SUMMARY

Army Form C. 2118

No 2

Place	Date	Hour	Summary of Events and Information	Remarks and references to Appendices
HERMAVILLE	5.iii.17	7.15 p.m.	Visited Advanced dumps near ECROIVRE. Inspected with Camp Commandant the 0 H/C 15th Royal Scots — ARRAS — interviews Town Major & Sanitary Officer. Inspected billet recently occupied by 25th D.L.I. Visited St CATHERINES — returned to Hermaville.	O.A.S.
HERMAVILLE	9.iii.17	7.15 p.m.	Visited ROCLINCOURT. Remained a member of ORP near Wellington street — interviewed M.O. of 2.5 D.S.T. who were in occupation. N. 2/Lt Sector of trenches — Visited ST NICHOLAS / ST CATHERINES	O.A.S.
HERMAVILLE	10.iii.17	7.45 p.m.	Interviewed Town Major & Officer Commanding Billets — Rode to 6 & 7 Battalions near ECOIVRES Inspected Rode BETHONSART. Remained of (illegible) Sanitary Station — interviewed Cmdt Commandant 2nd/4th Royal Scots. O.A.S. lines etc.... interviews areas also	O.A.S.
HERMAVILLE	11.iii.17	8 p.m.	Interviewed Asst/Suffolk, 11th/6th Royal Scots — also lines etc... interviews Visited CHELERS, LA THIELOYE DIEVAL — ROCORT, MAGNICOURT & HOUVELINE inspected billet Interviews Aide de camp inspected. Interviews Town Mayor of DIEVAL.	W.S.
HERMAVILLE	12.iii.17	8 p.m.	Rode ST CATHERINES Inspected work done by are — visited ROCLINCOURT — Trenches is occupied — interviews R.O. of 2.5 R.S. & y 152 B. RFS shown recently R.I.R. Section	O.A.S.
HERMAVILLE	13.iii.17	6 p.m.	Visited X Advanced camps aint ECROIVRE — interviews M.O. of 11 Suffolk. Most Advance point inspection camps occupied by these Battns — inspected trench station at ECROIVRE which are supple tents, 2 x Advance camp.	O.A.S.
HERMAVILLE	14.iii.17	7.30 p.m.	Visited Royal Scots Officer of Trenches — inspected & 8th of 21st & 25 who are now in operations & discussed water supply & time part of trench — visited ST NICHOLAS from advance point air Pumping station — inspected work done by Sanitary Section at ST CATHERINES & Suffolk Latrine in ST POL - ARRAS road.	O.A.S.
HERMAVILLE	15.iii.17	7.30 p.m.	Visited CHELERS Inspected R.O. of 20 D.L.S. now 2/Col. 2/Col. BURIE — inspected latrine work done in villages — visited LA THIELLOYE No. 12 C.C.S. — now 2/Col. BURIE — inspected ambulance in premises of Sanitary	O.A.S.
HERMAVILLE	16.iii.17	7 p.m.	Visited X Advance at D'ECOIVRES, inspected camps occupied by 10th Kiddy, m/c Suffolk; also Hotel Asy water tanks — Visited pumping station at ECOUVRES - inspected work done by Sanitary Section on ST POL - ARRAS road.	O.A.S.

WAR DIARY / INTELLIGENCE SUMMARY

Army Form C. 2118

No 3

Place	Date	Hour	Summary of Events and Information	Remarks and references to Appendices
HERMAVILLE	17.iii.17	7.30 p.m.	Inspected 34th R.E. dump at MAROEUIL, also 17th Corps Gable where troop of 36th Division are being on T. LOUEZ. Interviewed O.C. of 34th R.E. Visited HQrs of 10th Infantry Bde – Called at Headquarters 6th Div (ST AUBIN T LOUEZ) – inspected work done re course of construction at ST. CATHERINE, ST. NICHOLAS and HAUTE AVESNES & made arrangements with 10th & 11th Inf. Bns. for preparation of Viaduct. Visited HAUTE AVESNES then billets for Indian Division was to Trench for ROCLINCOURT	W.D.
HERMAVILLE	18.iii.17	7 p.m.	Visited X Hutments at ECOIVRES near Instructions testing Party re Hutment receive at 221 Coy (R.M.) R.E. w/ HAUTE AVESNES repairs of Hutments having been done by Infantry. Satisfactory.	W.D.
HERMAVILLE	19.iii.17	7 p.m.	Visited ST NICOLAS inspecting work being done by Sanitary Section also at ST CATHERINE. Visited Hutments & inspected venereal arrangements at Rynmabat & Posts of BOSKY. Inspected L.O. 27th R.A.P. & inspected water, reason, report & camp. LAWRENCE AVENUE – tour Inspected by the Battalion	W.D.
HERMAVILLE	20.iii.17	7 p.m.	Visited X hutments re inspected work being done. Visited hutments prepared by A.S.C. 34th Div in main road & and east of HAUTE AVESNES Instructions etc.	W.D.
HERMAVILLE	21.iii.17	7.30 p.m.	Visited ST. CATHERINE & ST. NICHOLAS & praised re transfer Hospital R.A.P's in BOSKY, LAWRENCE AVENUE – CEMETERY ALLEY – Saw O. 10th Lecture & inspected venereal hospital & R.A.P. Scabs.	W.D.
HERMAVILLE	22.iii.17	7.30 p.m.	Visited ST CATHERINE & inspected lintels in Cottage between ST NICHOLAS fantaring work (4 hospital) Changed duty bed head & and provided all Baths at ST CATHERINE on Franks (R.A.P.) Rue SCARPE, arranged walls in ROCLINCOURT – Reported to A.D.M.S. re arr. of inspection use Cat CHANCE (A.D.H.S.) Col. DOBSON. C.R.E. 34th Div 2 ST	W.D.
HERMAVILLE	23.iii.17	7.30 p.m.	Visited LOUEZ & ST. AUBIN between last Forms large T. inspected a num of hutments etc. Trench Drainage at hospital CATHERINE & inspected work in Vauxhall Cottage & a number of points. Visited X hutments inspected water in found satisfactory arrangement	W.D.

1875 Wt. W593/826 1,000,000 4/15 J.B.C. & A. A.D.S.S./Forms/C.2118.

WAR DIARY or INTELLIGENCE SUMMARY

Army Form C. 2118

No 4

Place	Date	Hour	Summary of Events and Information	Remarks and references to Appendices
HERMAVILLE	24.iii.17	4.45p	Visited left sector of trenches, regards water supplies — Saw Lt.O. 22nd R.F. re visit various portions of trenches — visited R.A.P. in LAURENCE AVENUE — inspected with him trav on water supplies to ST CATHERINE — visited 102nd Fd at ab HAUTE AVESNES re arrgts O.C. (Capt IRVINE) made arrangement with E-S.S.O. for supplies / coal to further his duties while water station) at HAUTE AVESNES.	O.K.
HERMAVILLE	25.iii.17	7.45p	Visited HAUTE AVESNES. Made arrangement for distribs. 500 blankets for 102nd Fd Ambulance on 6 X hutment — inspected camp with Camp Commandant (interview Lt.O. of 21st Div.) re-distrib. 12 Bell tents & 10 X ice-kelas — instructed 6 P.B. men who had arrived for their camp, in their work — Viz 4 for Sanitary work — 2 to 4 Camp — 1 for water distrib. action & Supervision supplies. 1 for care of incinerators within no 4 Camp. — Rct R.O. ACQ & inspected camp occupied by Horse lines. 160 — B22 R.A. of 21st Div. Visited various hutt lines. HERMAVILLE attend Conference (Sanitary) at 3rd Army Sanitary Schd at ST POL. Visited various filth water supplies in ST NICOLAS inspected work done & in process for same.	O.K. O.K. O.K.
HERMAVILLE	26.iii.17	7.30p		
HERMAVILLE	27.iii.17	6p		
HERMAVILLE	28.iii.17	6p	Visited ST CATHERINE & ST NICOLAS saw Town Major re salvato plans for burial of horses & stores & guardians — also inspected various water supplies in sundries — provided latrines, inspected Sanitary arrangement at R.A.P. at BOSIKY & in LAURENCE AVENUE. returning inspected water supply at ROCLINCOURT with R.O. of 22nd 87r.	O.K.
HERMAVILLE	29.iii.17	6p	Visited ST CATHERINE & ST NICOLAS re-defect work of Sanitary Subsection — supplies water, supplies & burial (round) for burial horses — M. TINQUES & new Town Major.	O.K.
HERMAVILLE	30.iii.17	6p	Visited ST CATHERINE with O.C. 28th Sanitary Section (Capt. RAYNER) handed over the — Visited HAUTE AVESNES saw O.C. 102nd Fd sper Camp Commandant — Trade arrangement for hand over — Sanitary Sundries trade order arrangements. On to TINQUES & made final arrangements with Town Major regarding transfer of MQN.	O.K.

WAR DIARY
or
INTELLIGENCE SUMMARY

Army Form C. 2118

No 6

Place	Date	Hour	Summary of Events and Information	Remarks and references to Appendices
TINCQUES	31.iii.17	6 p.m.	Removed HQ. of 74th Sanitary Section to TINCQUES — Visited LA THIEULOYE & DIEVAL & inspected certain billets where trouble German prisoners had been rptd. Made arrangements for disinfection & preliminary contact.	O.O.S.

(Sd) Edward Clift = R.A.M.C.T.
O.C. 74th Sanitary Section

www.ingramcontent.com/pod-product-compliance
Lightning Source LLC
Chambersburg PA
CBHW081552160426
43191CB00011B/1904